BLACK
MAGIC

By Suzannah Knight

"One Million People Commit Suicide Every Year"
The World Health Organisation

Published by:
Chipmunkapublishing
PO Box 6872
Brentwood
Essex
CM13 1ZT
United Kingdom

www.chipmunkapublishing.com

Prologue - January 2006

I had been well for over two years, depression and mania had stayed away from me, but in just one moment all my fears came back..... My mother and I walked into café Davo, my head hung low, hoping that I wouldn't see anybody and nobody would see me. I knew a lot of people and I'm sure they knew a lot about me too. Café Davo was a continental plush café bistro, very Italian, stylish and sophisticated.

I felt, particularly uncomfortable in this nouveau riche select café, even though I'd been going in there since it opened twenty years earlier. My mother liked posing, god knows why when she was dragging me along with her. People always look at everybody who comes into café Davo and they examine their clothing and their faces, intricately determining their social status.

I hurriedly took a seat in the window and my mother sat opposite me. I could feel people lowering their newspapers and pausing from their conversations to look at me, everybody always did. I can't remember whether I was glammed up or looking like an indie kid but I guess I was semi glammed up because men were gaping at me.

A large bald man was sat to the left of me, three tables away but we could still hear the conversation he was having with a couple and a good looking forty something businessman. I knew Kojak, the bald man, from earlier visits to the café. I only knew him to say hello to although my mother knew him slightly better.

The forty something businessman started to eye me up, and once Kojak had bid good day to my mother I heard the businessman enquire upon who I was. Kojak replied to him in a booming voice that I was "an unemployed psycho".

The café went dead my mother cringed and I just wanted the world to swallow me up. Kojak had summed me up in all of two words… and it hurt, harder than ever.

The glorious days 1977-1996

If you think you are going to read a story about poverty and a hard childhood then you are wrong I grew up surrounded by riches in a loving warm and dedicated family atmosphere. I suppose our family was a little weird in the fact we only knew a few of our relations; my mothers parents, grandma and grandpa and my fathers widowed mother, mama.

We had no other relations that we knew so we had a small family. My brother and I were educated privately with the hope of great futures for both of us. It was our parents' dream that we went to university, they thought that university was the answer to everything.

All through my life I heard about university and how good it would be. My father worked hard as an engineer, building oilrigs in the North Sea. He has had a very successful career working for BP and Shell all over the world. My mother was a successful housewife and was proud of it..

My mother was on the floor, her arms and legs had been cut off and she was bleeding to death. Then I awoke. That was my earliest childhood memory, a dream or rather a nightmare. I don't remember life until about the age of three, and I only remember short clips about that. I remember dressing up as a tramp and playing with the flowers in the garden. I also wanted to be a hairdresser but I was told I could never be one of those.

I remember the day my brother was run over by a car outside our bungalow. There was a screech of car brakes; I remember that I dare not look because I instinctively knew it was my brother underneath the car. I ran into the house and stopped at the door clinging onto the kitchen towel rail. I called to my mum after a while and told her there had been an accident. I was in shock. I spent the night at my grandparents, whilst my brother and mum were in hospital. He was allowed home after a while, but he would have a scar on his forehead for life.

Apart from that, my childhood was romantic and happy apart from when mum sold our family dog because she said she could not cope with it... My father provided a lot of money and there was never a shortage of anything. We always had what we wanted.

When I was four we moved to Holland because of my father's job in the oil business and we had a very nice life. It was always hot and we spent our time at the swimming pool or doing exciting things like touring Europe. I started school at this time too and came back to England to be educated privately. It was an awful school and the only memories I have are bad ones. Once, I talked through a story and I had my hand smacked in punishment. I wet myself and then fainted on the floor.

The other memories are of being bullied constantly by two girls throughout lunch every day. Once I had my head knocked repetitively against a wall by a boy too. I do not have any good recollections of the time spent there, I remember crying a lot and not wanting to go to school in the mornings. I dreaded Sundays because the next day was Monday and school. My mother took me away from that school, she knew I hated it and sent me to an all girls convent.

At the convent I learned to love school until my father's job in Holland ended and he started a new one in France. My mother was going with him so I would have to board at the Convent. I spent my seventh year of my life in permanent tears and homesickness flooded my body so much that the school sent for my mother and said it could not continue. She had to come back to the UK to look after my brother and me who was also unwell with homesickness. My father came home too, took a job in Scotland, and commuted weekly. All returned to normal and I once again enjoyed my education.

By the time I was ten I had a pony and a dog and I was very content. I competed in riding activities and joined pony club. I had an active social life and a fulfilled existence. My life was my ponies as they multiplied in number, soon I had two ponies and then I had three and eventually I had four at the same time. As a young teenager, I was normal and had many friends and interests. Making friends was not a problem for me, and I was invited to many parties and social functions. I was best friends with a girl called Alice and we were friends right through our teenage days, until I started hanging with a more street savvy bunch of girls who were popular with the boys.

As I sit writing, staring out over the beautiful moor, I feel blessed. Blessed that one, I am staring out over the moor and two, that I am writing. Writing has given me an interest a hobby and an occupation. As I reflect on my life so far, fate has given me a collision course, a nightmare but a living one. When I go as far back as my childhood, I contemplate whether or not I was severely bullied or did I just bare the brunt of nasty childish behaviour. I will probably never solve that but what I do know my childhood and teenage years shaped my mentality and over sensitive nature.

I was never an overly happy child, in fact I was never really content. I hated school with a passion and became a studious hypochondriac. But what I was, and still am, really good at is taking something up, then dropping it - walking from one life to another, sometimes without ever saying goodbye.

It was amazing to leave school at eighteen, we were free, men looked at our beauty and the world was our oyster. On leaving school, I took the train from Aberdeen to Edinburgh to spend a wild few days partying in the great city, drinking cocktails in the cobbled old streets and nightclubbing in the dark student clubs. I was so cool I was not going to university I was going travelling. I had never wanted to go to university. I had had no interest in studying the UCAS book; I did not know my BSc from my BA, more commonly known as degrees in bugger all, especially those from English universities. I had already, grown up, I did not dream about student life. I had been getting drunk since I was fifteen, I had done all that, or so I thought. The world was at my feet and after having suffered two years of hell at boarding school in Scotland I was happy again, I was ecstatic.

I started my periods late at the age of fifteen, and with them came serious depression. I am glad though I never took treatment for it like Prozac or the contraceptive pill, I am glad I was pill free. Not like now. I do not live normally any more. When I left school in 1995, I had two and a half years of living normally left. Now I worry every time I have a drink whether one day I'll end up with Parkinson's disease, motor neuron disease or something else incurable, because I take strong pills the consequences and side effects of which, no one is really sure.

The depression had subsided and better still the weight I had gained in two years at boarding school went with it. I got a job in a nice pub in Darlington after leaving school. The clientele were rich and I was popular, something I had never been really before. I had never been a popular girl at school and when I say I was not bullied I suspect or know I was mentally abused especially in my teenage years. The girls I was friends with were all sexually liberated. We were acting out sex and the city, well before it's time, but it did not bring us glamour it only brought us branding as slags and slappers. We did not care, we were enjoying ourselves. We were liberated women using men just as men used women. Why? Because we had been hurt by men.

I had never had a successful relationship. They lasted a couple of weeks and in the end I was hurt, demoralised, and lacking confidence with men so it became easier to have one night stands. With one night stands there was little chance I would get hurt. However, the masses saw it differently and my reputation was notorious. It did not bother me, well it did deep down, I just moved on to a different place and new friends.

I was happy working in the pub and made many friends. One afternoon two men were drinking in the pub and they told me I looked like Dani Bear, they offered me a job as their secretary at their concrete firm. I took the job, earned a lot of money working at the firm and at the pub, my bank account was growing and soon I would be able to fund my travelling.

I am 5 foot 6; I have long blonde, thick hair. Some people say I look like Ursula Andress or Bo Derek, I do not think I do. I am thin now, what I will be tomorrow is a constant worry. Whenever I start a new pill, I have to be certain it will not make me fat. That would destroy me, it already has. I would say I border between anorexia and a paranoid eating disorder, but I like it that way. When I am thin I am happy, and the benefits of exercise are mentally uplifting. I would love to be a bitch, which I am when I have PMT but for the rest of the time I think I am quite nice. I have flaws but I now know everybody has flaws.

Towards September 1995, I applied to an agency in London for a job in the French Alps, working in a restaurant in a ski resort. I got the job. I was flying to Serre Chevalier in December. The excitement was un-containable. I bought a completely new wardrobe and was looking forwards to working more than anything else I had ever done before. A few weeks before I left, the agency rang to say my destination had been changed... I was going to Verbier in Switzerland, now I was frightened. I was going to the playground of the world.

I fitted in, there in Switzerland, funnily enough. I belonged somewhere, like I never did again, until now. Maybe it was my background. I am from a wealthy upper middle class family. I was privately and publicly educated. I had ponies and four holidays a year. I had all the clothes and toys money could buy, and I had love. I was on top of the world. I skied every day and I worked hard. My bosses were impressed with my management skills, they thought I was clever and intelligent. In fact, my bosses became my good friends, or even family figures like brother and sister.

Switzerland was the time of my life. I was carefree and popular again. The boys loved me in Switzerland and I had a gang of girls I was good friends with too. Our lives were skiing, working and partying hard in all the best nightspots in the area. Everything was right for me until one day, a friend called into the restaurant to talk to me; he told me straight to my face that I had psychological problems. How dare he! I told him he was an alcoholic. He did not like that. His comment hurt me.

By the end of five months in Verbier, it was time to move on; I have never been back. I fell in love whilst I was there; to a man called Leonardo I dreamed I would spend the rest of my life with him and have his children. However, he in turn would break more than just my heart. Our love was nothing more than an affair, but it will stay in my heart forever.

I earned a lot of money in Switzerland; the rate of pay is far higher than England and I had accumulated sufficient funds to travel around the world. I chose as my port of calls Bali, Australia, New Zealand, Fiji, Hawaii and the USA, each was better than the last. I was meeting a friend in Australia and we would travel together supposedly.

I met my friend but he was in a state of depression and home sick, I left him because there was nothing he wanted to do and he was most unpleasant to me, so I travelled on my own. My travels were a mixture of depression and self-help books, fun and trouble, mischief and bewilderment, loneliness and good company. Travelling is very destabilising and I longed for security, love and a stable unchanging environment. I longed for something but that something was not university life.

My parents had forced me into going to university thinking it was the beginning of everything. It is for most people. They were not university educated themselves and knew nothing of the politics of life there. Since fifteen I had been a heavy drinker, it had eased my pain and depression. I had experimented lightly too with cannabis since I was sixteen and had smoked it regularly especially in Switzerland and whilst travelling, but I had always had the sense not to touch anything stronger.

1996

The Air New Zealand flight from LA to London was due to arrive at London in twenty minutes, the tannoy announced that there was a message for Miss Suzannah Knight, I was to go to the British airways flight desk upon landing

The plane touched down on British soil and my instant reaction was doom and gloom. After a year travelling around the world, I was back. I made my way off the plane, got my bags, sneaked through customs with my Australian crocodile skin and a flick knife and went to the British airways desk. My mother had left a ticket to Teesside airport at the desk for me. It was opening time at the pub and I celebrated my arrival with a pint of lager. Everybody seemed depressed and miserable, maybe it was the weather? It was raining and misty, even though it was the end of August. My flight was called and I was back in the North of England, how lucky was I?

I did not settle back into life very well, travelling had changed me. I thought I was really cool when I arrived back in England; I was very happy and proud of myself for what I had achieved. Travelling around the world had been my lifetime's dream and I had done it and succeeded. High on life, not from all the marijuana I had sampled around the world, I settled back into life at home.

Home was a small village five miles from Darlington; we lived in a large red-bricked modern house at the edge of the village overlooking the cricket field.

Looking over the field always seemed bleak and empty especially in wintertime. It was the end of summer just three weeks before I was meant to start university. My friends had already done a year at university where as I had gone travelling, making some of them very envious. However, it would be me who envied them later on in life.

One of the first things I did was to ring my best friend Alice. Alice and I had grown up together since we were thirteen years old and we had remained the best of friends through thick and thin. We had even given each other anniversary cards to celebrate our first year of friendship. We had scared people rotten with tales of ghosts at school, we robbed the tuck shop, we set up business at school trading sweets, we cheated our way through the Duke of Edinburgh's scheme and a lot more, we were usually naughty and got away with it. We were the best of friends.

We started experimenting with alcohol at fifteen and usually ended up in a bad way after a bottle of gin or a day in the pub. Once Alice fell down a hill in York after drinking all day and woke up with scars all over her body, it was days before I remembered what had happened to her.

Every weekend was spent at one another's house, we saw every film that ever came out, listened to every new cd, bought the same clothes and shared a world of secrets and friendship. We had the kind of friendship that one would have expected to carry on through to old age, no matter what we went through in between. At seventeen, we had started smoking pot together and we had a regular pattern of getting stoned in the car and then hitting the nearest pub and sitting laughing all night somewhere in the Richmondshire countryside.

The first thing we did when I got back was to score some pot and go to the Spotted Dog pub and after a joint I showed Alice photographs of my travels. We chatted, laughed and caught up again as if I had never been away. It was great to get home to my family and friends, especially Alice.

I had been home for two weeks when my other best friend from boarding school invited me up to Edinburgh for the weekend. Hannah and I always got very drunk together, it was our mutual interest. We drank shit loads of anything, bought by anybody, we danced and pulled the best-looking men we could find. This ritual was usually followed by a shitty one-night stand and then worrying if we had again caught a sexual disease. This weekend was set to be the same as usual or so I thought. The Friday night was spent getting drunk in the grass market; we did not go to a club as we were going to a new dance club the next night.

We slept all day long when we were in Edinburgh together and only got up in time for the next Vodka at six o'clock in the evening. We got ourselves ready, as usual, and did our camouflage, makeup, and left for the pub. After a tour of the pub scene, we ended up at my favourite watering hole, the filling station on the Royal Mile, for cocktails. Then we walked to the club where we had planned to meet Hannah's brother and his friends. Hannah had left me when we reached the club so I stood at the bar holding my whisky and coke talking to some boys about nothing in particular. Hannah came back with a big smile on her face and asked me if I wanted to come to the toilet with her. I said yes, naively wondering what was happening.

This was 1996, club culture was at its height of popularity, and with club culture comes heavy drug use. Hannah took out two wraps and gave me one. I had never tried any drug other than cannabis nor had I wanted to. I had been offered things but had always been sensible. I took the wrap of speed! whiz! Amphetamine and copied her taking the drug dabbing my finger in the nasty powder and putting it on my tongue. It tasted funny, sharp like a very fizzy sherbet. I became overly anxious wondering what was going to happen to me, I drank another whisky and coke and waited.

I came up on the drugs. I had a surge of energy and the music seemed comprehensible and logical. The beat and the booming notes all seemed to come together and suddenly I was out there on the dance floor giving it everything. I was the greatest dancer in the world, I could move to the music. I did not want to stop. My body was moving in time with the music and it was great I was great, I thought that everybody must think I was great too. Every part of my body seemed to be able to move differently, as if it had been released from what it was before. Hannah's brother came over and asked if I was all right. I smiled at him and said I was fine. I'd never felt so good in my life. I was happy.

I did not see Hannah that much that night because I was so busy dancing. Afterwards we went to a house party and everybody started skinning up joints. I remember sitting silently in the corner all night paranoid even more than usual after a joint. My jaw kept moving and I really felt uncomfortable and suddenly tired. I asked Hannah if she wanted to go home, I did not feel that I fitted in with the crowd of people I was with. I had been away from England for a year and I found it increasingly hard to connect with anybody again. We left and I got a few hours sleep. In the morning, my father was picking me up on Princes Street. I left Hannah early, I felt dreadful somewhere between death and post mortem. I sat in the car all the way from Edinburgh to Darlington in silence sipping an orange revival drink. I think my father thought I was just suffering from a bad hangover.

As soon as I got home, I was on the telephone to Alice telling her about speed and how great it was. She invited me to Newcastle on Friday night to celebrate some of our friends returning to university. She decided that she would ask someone at college in Durham to get us some speed. She succeeded. Everybody thought little Alice was innocent but she was not.

We drove up to Newcastle and went to a Davey's new house in Gosforth. Davey was Alice and mines mutual friend, a good friend. The house they had moved into was horrible, a typical student dump. The thought of university made my skin crawl and made me want to get angry. Wasn't there something else to do instead of university? Why didn't we have apprenticeships anymore? I really did not want to go to university. I had taken no interest in the UCAS book what so ever.

Ever since I had turned sixteen, I lost any interest in studying, I only liked boys, alcohol, clothes and cigarettes. I still managed to obtain three A's, three B's and three C's at GCSE. I wasn't particularly thick and I also attained three C's at A level. Considering I had only crammed for 24 hours beforehand and had rarely been to a lesson it was pretty good. I did not know my BA from my BSc nobody had explained anything to me or maybe I just didn't listen. My father's retort had been "what's the point of her being educated, she's only going to grow up and get married." My school had also failed to educate me. I was completely and blissfully ignorant of anything and everything to do with university. Yet it was my parents and school who had pushed me into university, I should have never come back from LA and travelling, I had been offered all sorts of opportunities whilst abroad.

I had chosen to study at Birmingham University reading travel and tourism. It had sounded good and meant I would be able to travel the world again. I had always wanted to work for a magazine, and I fancied being a travel editor for Vogue or Elle in the future. I had dreams once; unfortunately, they had dissolved during my time spent travelling.

We left the dump of a new house and went into the city. We drank on the quayside and then went to Julie's nightclub. Alice and I secretly made for the toilets. I showed her how to take the white powder mixed with anything dealers could find handy. We came out of the toilets looking proud. I was not anxious, I knew what was going to happen to me and I could not wait to get high and onto that dance floor. We never really saw the others again that night apart from when they came over to dance. Alice was not the most natural of dancers but I think she had a good time too.

We went back to the new house in Gosforth and Alice and I stayed awake all night, smoking joints. I did not feel very well, I had never felt like this before. Birmingham was supposed to be the start of the rest of my life. My father was so excited when I started he had even bought me a star mobile phone. All our lives he had warned us about the perils of drugs, but sometimes you try what you are warned against just to be rebellious. I wanted something else; I was looking for something I did not know about. It had been part of my finding the inner me whilst travelling. I opted to look for something else and I found it, only it was a big black bag of trouble, which brought me to my knees. I had wanted to be popular that was all I had wanted. I blame the travelling for my inability to settle into life in Birmingham and my recklessness for my waste. I would give anything to be nineteen again and begin my studies all over.

My parents took me down to Birmingham in the car. My halls were brand new and very nice. I had a premonition and a dream before going to uni that I would walk in and immediately fall in love with a handsome boy and it came true. I settled in and unpacked. My parents left very happily and left me a case of fosters. I wandered into the kitchen and introduced myself to the other people on my floor. They seemed nice if a bit square. Then a beautiful boy walked in he had chin length black hair and was very regal looking. He immediately came over to me and introduced himself. I was lost for words but knew he would be mine. I gave him a Fosters, we started chatting, and we got on great. That night about twenty of us went to the pub.

Danny and I were inseparable. We kissed that night and the next and it was not before long I had moved into his room. I only ever went back to mine for a change of clothes. The sex was amazing I had never had sex like this before and I liked sex. Except we were making love. Danny was also a reefer head and he skinned up all the time. I was permanently stoned during the day. He was making me hash coffees, and I was doing all sorts of bongs. He even tried to set me up as a prostitute but realized I was not that sort of girl. He was not a pimp either, his mother was a GP and his father was in the navy, he was a public school kid like me. I soon realized he was a bad card but by then I loved him.

We went out every night too and I got drunk every night. Some of the other students noticed I was not well and kept asking me if I was all right or told me to sort myself out. I did not make friends with any other students only Danny, he was all I had. I never went to lectures. I went to one of every module all term but I did not think anything of it. I was either stoned, recovering from my hangover in bed or having sex. I did not understand the course anyway; it was over my head. I am artistic not scientific so what was I doing on BSc course. The other students did not like me I can see why now really.

I was taking speed on a regular basis perhaps two or three times a week. I could not settle and life was a mess. I kept disappearing from university. One weekend I went home, the next I went to Sheffield to see my brother, then I went to London. I took Danny to see an old friend from school in Leicester, Taddie, who was heavily into cocaine and was fun to be with, we took loads of whiz and partied the weekend away at Leicester University. I upset Alice that weekend because she too was in Leicester and I was supposed to meet her only I was too stoned and paranoid to ring and arrange to meet. Then Alice came down to Birmingham to stay and so did a good friend Ben.

I was only interested in having a good time. Which meant getting high and pissed? I had had it with uni so I went and got a job waitressing in the famous Ronnie Scott's bar. It was great serving the rich and famous pop stars and musicians, but it was not long before I had the beginning of my mental break down. It had been a hard night partying, I had had speed and loads of alcohol. I had decided to go to an accountancy class the next day in which I was busy writing to Madonna saying how much our lives were similar, when I began to cry. The other students had left me to sit on my own and I was sure they were talking and laughing about me. I could not stand it anymore so I jumped over the desks and ran out. That night I went to work and I broke down crying. No one not even I knew what I was crying about but I said it was the other students. I did not work there for much longer because I thought one of the customers had offered me £400 a night to sleep with them. I cannot really remember what happened but I walked out. I walked out on Danny too and I went home and said I was never going back. Danny snogged another girl whilst I was gone so I knew he was not serious about me. I loved him but I could not stand the pain of him not loving me so I left him.

Whilst in Birmingham strange things had begun happening to me. I was paranoid to death. I thought everybody was talking about me wherever I went. I thought the radio and the TV were discussing me. The other student's bitchiness did not help but the sky and the clouds were moving fast and I was beginning to believe in Vampires. Paranoia at its most serious had riddled my body and brain. I had mania.

When I got home, I was in such a state my family thought I had been raped. I did not have anything to tell them. I was too busy going out getting high in the nightclubs at home with Alice. My parents were worried about me from the moment I got home, On the train home from Birmingham I had broken down crying, about what I don't know, I think it was just the sheer desolation and confusion of my life. I went down the train aisle talking to people and crying. People were very supportive towards a lunatic girl and very nice. My mother and brother met me at Darlington station and knew immediately something was wrong with me. We went to a café and I was sure the two guys next to me had followed me from Birmingham and were talking about me. I was going mad literally. I went home and my paranoia did not ease. I cannot remember what I did in my time at home but I think my behaviour was really weird. My paranoia was about everything everyone said or did, it was all against me. Everybody hated me; everybody was being sarcastic, and mean to me. The story of my life.

I left Darlington to go to the only party I had been invited to that Christmas in London at Ben's house. I had bought a beautiful Kookai suit in turquoise to wear. Everything was all right really apart from me speaking in riddles to a lot of people. It was the first time I felt I did not fit in I felt inferior at the party to other people and I ended up dancing on my own watching flirtatious couples enviously. I did not have a great time I was not well. The next night was really weird Ben and I met one of his friends and we went out to party at the clubs in London except every where we went got closed down I thought it was because I was a super agent and they didn't like spies being let in to the clubs. After London, I went back to Birmingham to pack up my belongings. I ended up in bed with Danny again and partying as hard as usual. We declared that we loved each other very much, but knowing he had snogged another girl had finished it for me and I knew I had made the right decision to leave. I had nothing there, I had failed to make friends, I was a wild party animal who was manic and I think everyone knew it. My parents collected me from Birmingham. It was very traumatic leaving Danny, we were both crying I knew I would never see him again; I will always love him.

Usually before Christmas I have a lot of parties to attend, but apart from the one in London there were none that year, only a gathering of Alice's friends in a night club in Darlington which was not memorable and I was on another planet. Alice and I went to Tall tress in Yarm one night. We had bought some speed and were really excited about the night ahead. I danced all night like a goddess; I thought I was the greatest dancer in the club and I even had my photo taken for a magazine. We were chatted up by two men who worked at ICI and it was this night that I realised that my imaginary world was better than sex. I shunned men from now on, not in favour of women but just thought sex and men were boring, I was far more interested in my mystery world.

On the way home from Yarm we were stopped by the police, it was just a routine check because we were late, I had some cannabis on me which made me a bit paranoid, but they left us alone. That night in bed, I stretched out and suddenly I believed I was a princess. I was the missing Russian princess Anastasia. I truly deeply believed it; I went to bed that night full of awe for myself. Suddenly this rejected, immoral girl was something special. I was also pining for Leonardo, I imagined we would get married and live happily ever after. All my thoughts were centred on him.

On Christmas day, I thought I was being watched worse than ever. The spice girls had their number one hit and I thought they were singing the song to me. Overall, the day was quite nice, I was happy in my new imaginary world and I did not yet hate my parents. We were all excited about going skiing to Morzine, France as we did every year. Everybody was really looked forwards to it and waited all year long for the magical week abroad. I was taking Alice with me this year, she knew the family really well so it seemed logical. I was going to go with her in the summer to Majorca. Alice and I were busy planning going travelling together some time in the future too.

The holiday began well, we were out skiing early and the snow was great. Then one night my brother, Alice and I went out for a drink in the town. I got very drunk and was talking garbage, I had another drink and another and eventually I fell off my barstool. I had blacked out, but I do remember the face of my brother and Alice, they were terrified, shocked. I must have been sprouting an awful lot of scary rubbish. That was the night the holiday went wrong. The next day we were skiing peacefully, Alice and I took a chairlift together and she knocked me over at the top as we were getting out. I fell and really twisted my knee, so much so I had to return to the apartment. This suited me actually, because it meant I could drink alcohol all day long in peace and dream my dreams. My father took me to the doctors that night to get some medicine for my knee. I suddenly began thinking my father was a right pratt and began to hate him. In fact, I had begun to hate everybody I was on holiday with and I made it clear, I was really nasty to everyone. The next day alone in the apartment, I emptied my medicine for my knee into the bottles of vodka and gin that the family was drinking. I wanted to poison them and kill them. If they were not around, I would be free to live in my imaginary world.

The last contact I had had with the love of my life from Switzerland, Leonardo, was a phone call in Birmingham which had been all of about ten minutes, but suddenly I was pining for him again. He was all I wanted and I was sure he was going to come and find me here in Morzine. I was also being watched in the apartment, through a camera in the light. The spies were Swiss intelligence working for Leonardo's father and they were down below in the apartment beneath us. As I was pining for Leonardo, working out my Princess story I was also fathoming out the plans for the third world war that was about to happen. As I was a royal Russian princess, I was very important in the scheme of things. I had also figured out who my real father was, he was a man I had met in Switzerland one night, an old man who was a Russian prince. Now I knew I was adopted and I hated my real father even more because he was not my real father at all.

My mother discovered the empty medicine packets and then they found a residue on top of the vodka and gin. My father was livid and we had a full-scale row.

"I've given you everything you little bitch." He said, and hit me very hard on the face. I flew across the room and hit the wall. I got up everyone was watching and I marched out of the apartment. Alice followed me. I was crying but brushed the tears aside. I told Alice I was going to the Café Chaud to get pissed. We got ourselves some glasses of wine in the best café in Morzine, which plays bands, has wild nights, and sat down. It was not before long that four sexy Swiss guys were sat with us. Alice did not like it being chatted up, I still do not know whether or not she is a lesbian but I have my suspicions. I pleaded with her to stay but she said she was going back to the apartment. I stayed and had a great time with the boys. They took me to the nightclub.

I thought they'd come on behalf of Leonardo and were going to take me to Switzerland and into his arms, however I was wrong and when I got in that car to go to Switzerland it took me as far as the boy's hotel. I felt that they had cheated me and could not believe they had taken me to their hotel so I began to fight them and we ended up in a scrap from which I ran off before I nearly got very hurt. The nice boys had turned nasty on me. I ran and ran and took refuge in the entrance to a hotel where I spent the night awake and frustrated with my mind. My imaginary beliefs were not coming true and it was disappointing. The hotel owners found me in the morning and took me in. I was talking and behaving very strangely and then suddenly the apartment owner where I was living turned up and took me home.

I still was not skiing I was in the apartment drinking. I took walks out into the nearby country where upon everything that I noticed had a meaning to me, the birds symbolised something, as did somebody's car number plate, I was going mad fast. Then one afternoon I was laid on the couch in the apartment in the hazy hot winter sun when I fell into a trance. My real Russian father was at the door holding crystal necklaces for me, he was telling me Leonardo was coming. I could smell Leonardo; I could smell his raw body odour. Then I felt Leonardo come into the apartment with one hundred red roses for me. Something hurt in my stomach I awoke from the daze there was nobody there. My mind was playing tricks on me and unfortunately, I interpreted them as spiritual meanings.

I was now classing people in terms of rank, one was the best type of person, then two and so on until you got to shit. Alice was shit in my eyes now and on New Years Eve at the meal, I told her so. I completely slagged her off during the meal. How I hated everybody. They were not my family and I had better friends than Alice in my head, she was not worthy of being my friend. The next day Alice and I had a huge row in which she told me she hated me.

Another best friend, Nadine whom I had worked with in Switzerland was working in Morzine and before having left England I had rung her and arranged to meet her. She had known Leonardo so seeing her brought every memory of him back again. I was wanting to leave the apartment as my family had returned from their day skiing as I could not bear to be around them for very long, they annoyed me. Some how I caused a row and then I left fleeing like an escaped animal. I hurried down to the Hotel where Nadine was working and asked at reception to see her. Nadine came through and took me to her living quarters at the back of the hotel. We had a little chat and caught up but I was away on another planet and thought she was talking about me to her other friend who was in the room. I got up suddenly and walked from the room I could not stand it anymore. It was early evening and I went and sat in the snow across the other side of the road to the hotel. I sat there for ages, and then I went back to Nadine's quarters and sat at her door crying my eyes out and sobbing for Leonardo. I was a wreck. Nadine found me later on and phoned my parents. They came over fast and frog marched me home. They were now asking Alice if I had been taking drugs, I do not know what she told them. I have never seen my good friend Nadine again since that incident.

The next day I was well enough to ski. I set off with the family for a nice day skiing but as soon as they were out of site I suddenly thought I was in the military SAS, I could feel them all around me and I skied off on my own and took a funny route back to the apartment down a trail in the mountain. When I got back to the apartment the residents of the below flat were packing their car to leave. I was convinced I was being watched in the apartment by Swiss intelligence, and now I had found the people with the spy equipment. I shouted to them. "I've found you now, I know who you are. Tell him I love him." They looked at me funnily; I wanted to scream at them, I did not like the feeling of being watched.

On the final day of the holiday which I had ruined, and will never be allowed to forget by my family, my mother stayed in the apartment with me because I was drinking all the alcohol. Then we flew home, at the airport Alice who had had a terrible time told me she hated me and we had a screaming match. I was then convinced that MI5 would be at Heathrow to meet me and take me away where I could tell them everything I knew. I thought the third world war was going to start and I had all the answers and had met all the people who were going to organize it whilst I had been travelling. No one met me at the airport. I had a lot of hopes and expectations about what was going to happen; only they never did so I would get very frustrated and momentarily depressed, but then my imaginary world took over and I was happy again.

1997

When we returned home, the drinks cabinet was locked and I was locked in the house, but I was so high I did not need anything to aid it. My parents were worried and were watching me carefully. It has never been discussed whether or not there is mental illness in my family tree but I know a great aunt committed suicide years before using paracetamol. My mania continued, my parents tried to talk to me about my future, I did not want to know, I thought great things were going to happen to me without me doing anything to help. My mother dragged me down to the University of Leeds, to continue my studies there. I said no, I did not want to go. I could not stand the stress of going back to university, it did not interest me. She then dragged me to the chamber of commerce where I had an awful meeting with an old man. He knew I was not interested in the course on offer and he told me so. It was an awkward and embarrassing moment. So I signed on the dole, and when I had to go for job interviews I messed them up.

I had ruined my family's annual ski trip. They thought I was just being a brat, they did not know there was something wrong with me and they did not want to admit to themselves that there was anything wrong with me. I was still manic and my parents knew it, my father had turned my room upside down looking for drugs, he thought I was taking heroin. The front door was always locked as was the back so that I could not escape as I had done in Morzine. It was for my own good, I always seemed to get into trouble when I escaped. Moreover, all the time my parents were trying to protect me from myself, and keep me away from the authorities. When I was sat in my room, I thought I was with members of the English SAS who then developed into members of the elite group made up in my mind of the Belize soldiers. I stole some cans of lager from the fridge and drank them with my new soldier friends. It was the same feeling of military that I had had whilst skiing. It was not as though I came from a military orientated background but the connection with the army reigned right through my illness.

When I was not in my room imagining whatever I imagined, I was down stairs in a massive row. I was taken into the kitchen with my parents and my brother, who had stuck his nose in and was questioned about things I didn't want to be questioned about. A huge row would peruse to which I did not understand why. It seemed that my parents were constantly rowing and I was in the middle, although I was the cause. I wish I could remember what the rows were but I cannot, although now I know they were over my strange behaviour. I remember being very objectionable and talking about weird things at dinner times, I would cause a row to erupt after I had caused trouble, usually by being very nasty and rude. I was still under the illusion that this family was not mine and all I wanted was to be with my made up fantasy family. I wished this family were dead. Life was not exactly perfect I had no close friends especially as Alice was not talking to me after the ski trip. I never bothered to ring her, as far as I was concerned she was still a piece of shit. I had new friends; they were all that mattered. I was going nowhere fast.

It was a dull January day; the view out of my bedroom window was as lonely as ever. We lived in a village yet I knew no one in it, I often thought that was not very normal yet there were a lot of things about my family life that I did not find very normal, and they were thoughts I had since being a little girl. I hated my family for what they had made me, for the things they had made me do. I had never excelled at anything and I blamed them for that too. I blamed them for never buying me the best pony, for sending me to boarding school, for not having enough money, and for everything that had gone wrong in my life.

Alice came around one day with her mother. I expect my mother was very embarrassed as to what had gone on holiday although we have never discussed what she said to Alice's mother that day. Alice came up to my room to talk. I was sat on the bed waiting for the great things to happen to me. We spoke, me with authority and delusions and she normally. Then she went, if I had only realized I would see her four more times in my life I might have been different towards her. I just sat on the bed and regarded her as trash; I had not the faintest bit of interest in her and was really quite rude. At this time there was no rationalizing with me, nothing mattered to me and nor did I care. I was completely selfish in my objectives, nothing was important except me. I think I really upset Alice and hurt her although she has hurt me more since. I suppose looking back though I did not deserve to have her as a friend I got rid of her as if she was indispensable I pushed her away and our friendship in favour of my mind's tricks.

The time I spent in my room was consumed by spending time with my make believe friends, people I had met around the world. I was having conversations with them in my head. I could feel them all around me. Then god came one afternoon and told me in my head, I was not hearing voices yet, to get my address book. He then told me to pray that every body in the book should die and that I would never speak to any of them again. Well he was right although it was that none of them would speak to me again. I tore up the address book at his command. It was at this time that Leonardo's spirit also entered the room; he sat besides my pine wardrobe and watched me, telling me he was coming to see me. I could see the faint outline of his body, he was such a large man, his spirit was black, and sometimes it brushed my body.

I was still pining for him and that is when something miraculous happened. I lay in the bath each afternoon soaking up the bubbles and smoking cigarettes I had nothing else to do and it was very relaxing, when all of a sudden I found myself connecting with a spirit or rather a person. In my head, I began talking to a man who at first reminded me of the bad guy in Bangkok Hilton. He had very dark hair and was very much a James Bond figure. He was incredibly beautiful; I knew exactly what he looked like, as a picture in my head was visible. You see when I closed my eyes I could hallucinate and his image came to me on this wonderful afternoon. He was full of life, and also, very rich. The first thing he said to me was that he would never fall in love with a girl like me. I was talking to the imaginary character for ages. He said he was in the Kings Head hotel in Richmond watching me.

He was with the navy and was going to be an ambassador of Morocco one day. He swore to send me a package of cigarettes and booze. Every day I waited by the door for the arrival, it never came. However, he came back to my mind every day. He made my life worth living and I got to know him better and better. At first, he had seemed quite evil but now he was nice. I could sometimes feel his spirit in the house moving around, the house had become haunted. Dark shadows would appear on the hallway and on the stairs. I could hear things in the loft and in the next-door rooms. Black shadows fell and rose throughout the house. Every night Piers told me that there was a helicopter coming for me to take me away as I was so special. Every night I waited by the window ready to climb out when it came but it never did. Piers told me to do naughty things, he spoke to me when I was doing things and made me laugh. It was like having an imaginary friend. There was that film once with Rik Mayall as the illusionary friend it's title was Drop Dead Fred, Piers was like that to me, he was every where I went and he affected everything I did.

I never had an imaginary friend as a child but I got one in adult life. Piers even dictated what I wore, because I thought he was watching me all the time I thought he could choose what clothes I bought. We went to House of Fraser one day and he told me to buy the long cardigan and the striped skirt... I even chose a wedding dress for him as we were falling in love. I was experiencing feelings I had never had before.

Piers told me to run away, he now dictated my life, and my life was now dedicated to Piers. If I ran away, god would get rid of my mother and my brother, Piers told me he was going to kill my father too in Scotland by giving him a massive heart attack. Piers told me I had to wait until we all went out though. One afternoon my mother said we were going to Richmond for a walk and a look around the shops.

On the journey there, I was having thoughts that my brother and mother would be killed in a car crash at Scotch Corner if I left them. If I got rid of them, I would be free to be with Piers. As soon as we got to Richmond, I was planning my escape. I waited until they went into a shop and then I ran. I ran to the castle and along the narrow winding path around it. I rolled down the embankment to the river and ran across the bridge. Then I found myself in a field and it began to rain so I sheltered in a barn for a while. I then followed a path to Easby Abbey I did not know where I was going but then I thought I could go and see Sally who lived at Easby. I found my way to her house and knocked on the door. There was no answer so I took cover in her shed. It was raining hard and I was soaked, I was sure my brother and mother would be dead by now. I sheltered for ages and then Sally opened her door and invited me in.

Sally was a girl with whom I had worked with in the pub when I had left school. I must have been relatively normal because she did not think anything strange and offered for me to spend the night. My mother had figured out where I was and she rang saying she would pick me up in the morning. That night we watched the terminator and I then slept on the sofa. It was here I first experienced black magic. The serpent was talking to me whipping me in half and talking about sand. He was negotiating sand from his Arab principality in exchange for me. I had military thoughts and thoughts of the devil and the werewolf. The whole air around me seemed magical thick with mystery, it was something I had to be part of it excited me like nothing had before. It was a mist of new beginnings in which I was going to live in high society, life would be full of fashion shows, cruising, balls, trips abroad, life in London and glamour and love. I had the world at my feet and I would be a black magic woman. I returned home in the morning, god knows what Sally had thought, I never saw her again for a while, and she never rang. I went back to my bedroom and talked to vampires who visited me at night, and I waited patiently for the military helicopter to take me away.

One day I went up to a private gym, my mother had membership, and I remember thinking that I was an undercover James Bond woman. I was there for a clandestine meeting with a spy. I thought there was a spy in the sauna to whom I was passing messages telepathically. The poor man must have been scared out of his mind, yet I do not think I did anything irrational. Another time I went to Richmond and believed I was a town planner through the black magic. I was going to make Richmond the place to be like a tourist trap. I ended up in the pub that day drinking on my own and I met a guy called Tony, he was friendly if not a bit scary. I was not really in the mood for socializing as I was busy writing cards and letters to people I had met whilst travelling about black magic. I never had any return post.

As my mind lost track of the black magic it returned to thinking about Leonardo. I began to feel his spirit in my room; I could see him stood behind the pine wardrobe door. One day I went for a walk with him in the country, he was with me every step I took, like a black shadow.

I had not been in contact with Leonardo since a telephone call in Birmingham apart from the spiritual connection I had started to imagine and hallucinate, and then, out of the blue in late February, he rang me. He said he was in England and could he come and stay. My mum said it was all right and I lay in wait for him. His arrival confirmed that all my thoughts were true and I had actually been in spiritual contact with him. I was very anxious about him coming to stay and meeting the parents. I believed he was coming to ask for my hand in marriage. I fell into his arms when he arrived and never wanted him to leave me. The first night was very strange here was I believing black magic was happening to me and Leonardo took a torch, shone it in my eyes, and said "Believe in magic" which was peculiar and fit in with my thoughts, and it again reconfirmed my belief. He also went on and on about Hitler and was heil Hitlering down the road one day, which again reinforced my beliefs about the third world war.

My parents were not particularly keen on Leonardo and kept him at arms length. During the course of the weekend, we went to restaurants and into Darlington, and went to York for the day too. Leonardo was going travelling to South America where he was going to find work. He wanted me to go to, but I did not have any money and my parents said I could not go and would not lend me any money. He left as soon as he had come. I do not think I acted with much mania that weekend or at all strangely but I never heard from him again. I do not think my parents were rich enough for me to marry into his family either, from what he gauged from our home and material goods. I knew he had gone and I would never see him again so I got on with my life whatever that was for me now.

My parents wanted to know what I was going to do with my life. My father kept saying it was going down the tubes but did little to help. . Suddenly my life had a meaning, black magic. I was the missing Russian Princess Anastasia and sooner or later, the world would find out who I was so my future would be all right. I really believed I was her.

I did some really weird things during this period. I wrote friends and acquaintances strange letters and sent cards to them and weird stuff, I never had any replies. I had actually come down a lot and was getting a little saner. It was the end of February and it was depressing weather. I had seen Alice only once since I came back, she did not ring anymore. Ben rang me and asked if I wanted to come up to Inverness for the weekend. I said yes. I decided that on the way I would stop in Edinburgh with another old friend, I really made a fool out of myself staying with him, I cannot remember what planet I was on but it was not a good one. I have never heard from him again either. I was losing friends like those men that were shot down in the 1st world war. I had scored some pot before I left and had it tucked secretly away. It was on the train I met Piers Windsor for real, in an imaginary sense.

Everything had a meaning again to me, and people all knew me, they were all significant in the structure of my mania. When I got to the hotel in Inverness I booked in, I was a royal princess. I unpacked and had dinner. There was a Fijian man who said hello to me, he knew me from when I was in Fiji he had come to see me. After dinner and a few pernods, I went to my room and had a joint, and then the black magic happened to me. There was a wizard, a werewolf, a serpent, the devil, god, and the Fijian man who was a sorceress and I the princess and Piers Windsor the MI5 guy who would report the black magic to the government.

We organized world war three and other things. I had arranged the war, I would be so famous but undercover infamous. I had been the missing link in the magic circle and now they had found me. The night was heavy the air was thick it really was black and the spirits came evil, then good, then evil. I stayed awake all night and felt the black magic around and in me. I did not know anything about black magic but I did now.

I never met Ben that weekend, he had been trying to meet me but I did not leave the hotel room, it was great to get high and be on my own. On Monday morning, I left Scotland, higher than ever. Piers travelled with me all the way, we were good friends now, but I think we were beginning to fall in love properly.

One afternoon in February, my mother called me down stairs and said she wanted me to see somebody. A psychiatrist had arrived. I knew him he had helped with my birth, when I had been secretly brought into the country from Russia. He asked me some questions, but he did not seem too alarmed and he left. However, it scared me it really scared me. I did not know anything about loony bins or the nuthouse, but he had scared me. It brought me down to reality really and the mania seemed to go away. A social worker came to see me and told me I was having delusions of grandeur and I had to fit into society and get a job, I told him to get lost.

After February, I had one period of mania when I felt the royal navy was watching me in the shower one morning. The weird thing was there was a royal navy articulated wagon parked only a few miles away from the house that morning I discovered when I went out. And so I was in the navy now, undercover.

It was later in the month I realized that on my clean medical record I now had a behavioural disorder. I had been at the doctors for something routine when I had glanced at the computer screen and read my files.

I saw a couple of friends in March before my depression, Ben came down and we met Alice. I slagged her off all night to Ben in front of her whilst we were out in Harrogate for the night. I had a joint with Ben later when Alice had gone and we were back at my house, but I could not contact Piers Windsor. I thought if I had a joint, I would be with him. I saw a couple of other friends and acted bizarrely there too with them, but on the whole, I did not do anything or go anywhere.

I was losing more friends as my episode of mania went on, soon everybody would be able to gossip about my mental state. My mother dragged me down to London to see an educational psychiatrist who said I should study fashion because of the clothes I was wearing, I did not want to know, but I wish I had listened. I thought I saw Piers Windsor's friends that day in London, I was still manic.

But then the mania went away and I came back down to earth with a bump. I became seriously depressed. I did not want to go out. Do anything, or see anybody. I stayed in bed for almost six months, sleeping all day. I began a home study course in

Freelance Journalism and passed with Honours, but when I look back, my work was centred on all the thoughts I had had in the past six months, so it was rubbish really. I was pleased, but when I applied to the local paper for work, I did not get anywhere so I gave up, what was the point. I was depressed, introverted and uninterested in life. I did not want to live anymore. All I saw was black and nothing in the future. My dreams had not come true, black magic and Piers had failed me and left me alone. No one rang me and if they did, I did not want to speak to them. Nadia called once, I said I was having dinner and would call her back I never did. Nobody else rang.

My birthday came, and with it no cards. I had no friends anymore, I had nothing. God had told me to tear my address book up one afternoon during my mania and told me never to speak to anybody ever again, and if I prayed they would all die. I felt a little better in the June and decided to visit a friend in Newcastle for a night out, but I was fat, I had grown fat. During my sleeping and depression I'd been eating everything and had gained two stone. I covered myself up I was ashamed; I liked being thin, very thin. During my mania, I had been very thin and very beautiful, now I was fat and ugly. I went up to Newcastle in baggy clothes. I was not interested in alcohol now but I still got very pissed and made a complete fool out of myself dancing manically, I thought I was going to be picked to be a pop star or a dancer. I never saw my friend again and I did not go home with her either, I met a boy that I had known and kissed in Fiji on my travels which was totally mad. I went home with him and spent the night with him. I cannot remember what happened because I had a black out, but I caught scabies.

The trauma of the disease was very upsetting. It made me bed ridden again. I began sleeping all day and getting up in the evening and exercising like crazy. Then I read books all night. I also contracted trichotillomania. The pulling of hair from your head, and I ate it. It really is the most disgusting and shaming physical condition but I could not stop doing it, I enjoyed it. Most people would be bald by now but my hair is very thick and grows back quickly. Sometimes I would have bald patches and uneven bits of hair. It is an impulse control disorder.

I felt like doing something by August, I was thinner and happier, I wanted to semi live again. Two friends from Switzerland contacted me and asked me to go to Greece. I was going to and then I did not. I have never seen them again either. Then I decided to apply for a job through the agency I had been with in Switzerland to work abroad again. I got a job, thought about it, and chickened out. I did not have the mental energy to sustain working abroad. I could not be bothered with life anymore. I wanted to go abroad but I also knew I had to get a degree.

I got in contact with an old friend at the end of summer, June. I had been to the Convent with her. We started going out for a few boozy nights, and then I told her I had believed I was a princess and all about the black magic. She had been my best friend for years so I thought I could confide in her but I turned out to be wrong. She looked at me as if I was crackers. In fact, she would spread a rumour I was schizophrenic. I took a job at the local pub, it was very quiet and boring, I did not meet anybody and I used to sneak drinks in the afternoon, when nobody was around. Alice came in one night with her sister, we did not say a lot to each other, she was distant and cold, not like the old Alice, she told me she was going to Glasgow to live and I said I was going to Cambridge. I had applied for a business studies course at University of Anglia in Cambridge, the reason I picked the course was you got to the spend two years in Holland, that suited me, I couldn't wait. I arrived in Cambridge late September, just after Princess Diana's death. I had been very saddened by this and began reading in detail about her.

I needed to escape from Darlington; there was nothing there for me. With there being no university nor employment the middle classes all leave at eighteen and never come back leaving the town desolate and only returning at Christmas time to see their families. My friend in Switzerland had been to Anglia University in Cambridge and it seemed a nice place to go. I had been there before when I was very young and remembered it being a magical place. I had had a lonely summer although I could have done things, but I knew I needed to get a degree, however was that why I really went to Cambridge? At the back of my mind I still believed in the Black magic, I believed Piers Windsor existed. I thought that if I went to Cambridge I would be near to the secret intelligence in Britain and would for certain meet Piers, after all he had told me he had been to

University there. I also went to Cambridge with the light of reality that I would meet a rich young man who would marry me, but more realistically, I wanted to get away from home. Leave the claustrophobic love and protection, the inane rows, and the panic over my well-being. I really did not think about what to study and just chose business studies, I had done it at GCSE and had been good at it and it seemed a useful degree to have.

I went to university with the energy and focus on doing things. I planned to join some sport societies and even theatre group. I had plans and inspiration again, I was even looking forwards to socialising again, which had been along time in coming, my depression seemed to have lifted.

My parents took me down in the car to my private apartment in a student block. The rooms were small with an en-suite bathroom, and communal kitchen. We did not meet any other students so they left me alone in my little room. I would see them in three weeks time as we were going to France for a weekend holiday. It was a long time before I met anybody. I wandered around Cambridge taking in the amazing architecture and pizzazz of the late summer in the beautiful city. The halls began to fill up and I met a load of other residents. The first social activity that was planned was going to the student union for a drink. I had not drunk in six months and was very apprehensive. I began drinking pernod, it was cheap and chic.

For two weeks, I cannot remember going to bed. That old feeling of waking up with a hangover was back and then trying to remember what I did in my blackout came back to taunt and haunt me. I tried to stay in but I was bored, what was there to do apart from going out and getting pissed. Lectures had not begun yet and besides I did not want to miss out. There were no nice boys which was a disappointment I really needed male company. A Greek guy had fallen in love with me but unfortunately, he had a hunch back and was really quite ugly, shame because from all accounts he was rich. My aims to join societies went as far as going out on the preliminary pub-crawl, and no further.

Lectures began two weeks after arriving. I had my timetable, my books and I was a zealous student. I went to every lecture and listened, but unfortunately, I got no work done. I really could not do it. In my two years away from studying, my brain had become lazy and damaged, it did not work as it used to. I tried to do the homework but failed at every attempt. I had a pile of work I just could not do. I remember being in lectures and not having the faintest idea what anything was about. It was completely over my head and I was scared. I was doing French as a side subject too and even that was hard. I was at the bottom of the class with not a hope of passing no matter how hard I could have studied. What was worse was that the other students were flying through it whilst I did not even understand the names and words, references and logistics of the subject. Therefore, I was achieving nothing very quickly. At eight weeks, I gave up going to lectures and began to party harder than ever.

I had not really bonded with any girls in the apartment there were a few but our friendship seemed to wilt as my problems grew larger. I had bonded however with three boys. One boy was the Greek, another boy was a boy I had been at sixth form school with and the other boy was someone I used to my advantage Galvin. With the Greek, I partied at exclusive nightclubs, and dined out with him. I painted, played games and watched movies with him. Looking back, I should have married him as he kept asking me to. I would have had a nice pad in Holland Park and Cyprus, but he just wasn't good looking enough for me, only now could I marry just for the money alone. My old school friend was someone I again dined out with but also played pool with, nights were spent at the local snooker club and I actually got quite good at the game. My old school friend was lonely and it was nice to see a pleasant face from the past. Then there was the friend Galvin, whom I used to my advantage and was my partner in crime. We first met over a pint in the student union.

I had a broken family behind me caused by my behaviour I had a degree going nowhere and I had broken all social contact with my former friends, I felt like I was in no mans land with nothing. If I had had my head screwed on I would have followed my dreams and gone to London and worked in a swanky bar or club but I didn't I followed devils advocate and took that spliff from my partner in crime in my apartment one afternoon. My partner in crime, was from Stanstead, a grammar school educated boy, and a pot, speed head with a taste for alcohol. Our afternoons became full of drinking Stella Artois in the pub or at my apartment; I had found my nemesis although the sex was not there. We had no sexual relationship only a plutonic one. Yet he still probably hoped for one, and was still keen to dish the drugs and alcohol out freely. We egged each other on, whether it was the next pub, the next wrap, or the next joint. Life became a myriad or pub crawling, bongs and Stella Artois cans, it helped me to forget. And eventually it took me to my other world, the world I had come to Cambridge to be in.

And then Piers returned, I was hallucinating very badly by this time. I had turned my room into a black magic shrine, there were books and posters with black magic on and I was practicing rituals. The weird thing about my black magic was that it was actually written about in some of my books, the characters that had appeared to me were down on paper so I knew it was all true. That was the manic thing I was having a psychotic period and it was actually recorded in history, which added to my dementia. I could see Piers in my room, he was kneeling down with a ring in his hand and we were engaged. I put my ring on my left finger. Christ he was everywhere in spirit I could see him in the street in the halls when I visited friends, he was everywhere. I could see his outline and his suit and I could see the smoke form his cigarette, it curled as it gently floated through the air. He told me his life story and we dreamed of our life together in the future.

At this point in my time down in Cambridge I had not returned home or contacted my parents a lot, I had enjoyed a brilliant weekend in France with them at the beginning of term but after that, I did not see them. I have no time scale of when anything happened either. My psychosis was taking over I was becoming a loner and my friendships were ending where as most peoples were taking off. I found it difficult to interact with the girls and I had more boyfriends. I was getting on well with my old school friend and as yet, that friendship had not been damaged. I had had heard a rumour about him before I came to Cambridge, seemingly he had gone mad in Australia on acid and had been exiled and mental institutionalized, every body had stopped speaking to him. It did not bother me he was a friend. One night I kissed him, I had been tidying his room for him, when I found a black magic tin this set me off on one, and it meant he knew about my black magic. I began to cry and say it was not my fault it happened they made me do it, and then I passed out pissed. I had been quite hysterical. I suddenly thought I was going to be prosecuted for having been involved in Black magic.

My friendship with the Greek was growing strength by strength too and I will always remember him. We were good friend but I just did not fancy him although I loved him, he had a hunch back and a crooked nose. However apart from having Galvin, the old school friend and the Greek as good friends I was becoming a loser and a loner nights were spent in with a joint and a bottle of vodka, every night, I liked being with my imaginary friends.

The snakes came all over my body, I was like the Bond girl Solitaire in Live and let die. There were serpents everywhere, I could feel them crawling over my body. There were wild animals in my room, there were bugs. I was bad. One night I was really physically ill, it was my head it felt like it was being split, the brain was about to break into little pieces. I was ill, angry and frustrated. I had been getting up every morning expecting to meet Piers and he never turned up, but he visited and tried to kill me in the shower every morning for a joke. I wanted to get on with my life with him.

It was nearing Christmas and something odd happened to me. I was in my room when I thought the IRA had planted a bomb to kill me so I ran from the apartment block in a James Bond commando style. I kept running down the street until I reached central Cambridge, it was dark so I thought I'd go for a drink in Pizza express, I was sat on the sofas, the restaurant was quiet, two men entered the lounge area and said "There she is." They came over and sat with me. They were young in their thirties, respectable men, intelligent and authoritative. We hit it off straight away, and they bought me drink. Then we all went to a nightclub. I do not know who the hell they were or what they wanted, but looking back I think they were mental health nurses who had come to check me out, they had obviously come looking for me, unless the restaurant had called them, I do not know.

Some nights I felt black magic but mainly I was just with Piers. I started going out to restaurants and bars on my own because I thought he was going to meet me there. I don't know what I did whilst I was sat at the bars and at the tables but I hope I didn't talk to myself Sometimes I went out with ghosts, they were my friends, sometimes I went out with the devil. I also had begun to spend money, a lot of it. I liked shopping a lot. I bought expensive clothes and ornaments. I found a black magic tin in the chocolate shop and thought it had been made for me to celebrate my connection with it. The reason why I was not practicing black magic anymore was because I was friends with the entire magic circle now; they had all accepted me and were introducing me to more friends. My best friend was the sultan of Brunei's father, he changed into a dinosaur after midnight he was my grandfather because I was the missing Russian princess. The worst thing that I did during this period was to cut myself. I thought that every nation I had visited during my time spent travelling had implanted bugs into my legs through food I had eaten, and one night I got a Swiss army knife and cut myself open trying to find the bugs. There was blood everywhere and to this day, I am scared very badly.

In reality, nights were spent laughing with my Greek friend he took me out all over the place. We laughed and laughed and really got on even though I was completely manic. I could have been a very rich Mrs.

Stenapoulousoukoulous by now if I had been sane. I met Galvin some afternoons at the locomotion and the Kings head pubs we always drank strong Belgium beer by the pint. One afternoon a nutter came in the pub and sat with us Galvin knew him. Galvin turned to me pointedly after he left and told me he had just been released from the mental institution. I cringed, what the fuck sort of place was that? The only thing I knew about mental asylums was the one in the film Midnight Express, when the protagonist goes psycho and ends up in some weird part of the prison.

My old school friend and I were still playing pool most nights, I was an ace at pool and we started betting money, and drinking loads. I liked my old school friend even though he had called me a weirdo when I had first met back up with him, we got on great, and I missed him after I left Cambridge. I felt sorry for such a normal and kind boy to have lost his mind and who had been punished by all his friends turning against him and not speaking to him because he had gone a little manic. There was nothing wrong with him.

The end of term had approached everybody had left. The owner of the apartments had rung and told my parents to collect me; I do not know what else he told them. The day before they arrived, I was tripping, not on acid just in mania, I went out onto the roof, and it was like a balcony. I thought about jumping because there were all these wild animals in my room and they were after me. As I leaned over the edge, I fell back suddenly and hit the balcony floor. I shit myself literally, out of fright in my jeans.

My mother and my brother collected me on Christmas Eve. They were not in a good mood. My mother found my jeans, packed my bags and things and we left. They lost the three thousand pound deposit on the room because seemingly I had broken the shower. I had not; it had broken because it was crap. However, no one believed me. I had also stained the floor with red wine and ruined the mattress because I had pissed it so much through being drunk. The most embarrassing thing about having been in Cambridge was that there was an Asian girl on my floor opposite my room. She shagged her boyfriend who lived next to me every night and the noise was unbelievable, you could hear their lovemaking two floors below and along the corridors, there must have been a lot of complaints... Everybody thought it was me; I know this because a German Guy asked if it was me, I said no it was Caita. No one believed me. I got mucky looks from everybody.

The only thing I hope is that the next term she did it so everybody would know it was not me. The journey home was filled with fury. My mother was ashamed of me, she knew I had not been to uni and as yet, they did not know how I was mentally. I cannot remember much about going home only I spent a lot of time in my room. My mum and brother found a bag of anis herb powder and thought it was heroin, it was not. I had lost my mothers gold jewellery and they thought I had pawned it for drugs.

I was in the shit. I was giving my brother a mouthful so he hit me on my nose, it broke. I wanted to kill him; I wished the whole family were dead. The annual ski trip was booked. I did not want to go, I pleaded with my parents not to let me go. I did not I stayed at home with my grandma who lived with us.

I was fully psychotic. I was hallucinating very badly. They were so vivid and beautiful. Piers came into my room in a coffin one night. He then stood up and came over to my bed, and laid on top of me I could feel his manhood pressing against me as I looked into his eyes. Then he disappeared in a flame of smoke through the wall. Jesus also came into my room and he lay on top of the wardrobe, so did King Richard the lion heart. During the day the Nazis were killing the shit and burning them, I could smell it in the air.

I stole my brother's car and drove all over the place. I went to Richmond one afternoon and drank in the Buck pub. There was a tall man at the bar Tony who I had met before, quite a good looking forty year old. He sent me a glass of wine over and then came to chat to me. He was different but I was a little scared of him. I left, who would be to know that I would one day live with that man for four years. I also took an old friend, June out. I picked her up and took her to Harrogate, we got pissed. I remember her face as I laced into her about black magic. She was terrified. She also could not believe I was drinking and driving. I have never seen her again. I beat my grandma up too; we had a fight because she took the car keys away from me. She fought back though I do not know why I was blamed for the whole fight.

There were vampires in the house, and the sultan of Brunei's father was making me crazy. I was having a great time I looked forwards to each day. I stayed in most of the time drinking and living in my imaginary world, it was better than real life. I spent New Year's Day on my own with a bottle or two of red wine. I had nowhere to go and nothing to do; I watched films and played with my things in my bedroom. No one rang me sent me any cards or invited me to a party. Nor would they contact, ever again in the future.

My parents returned and I think there were a great many rows. Furious rows, where I would be locked in the kitchen and made to talk. What about? I was not about to tell them about all my secrets. My psychosis had made me very violent because I was so frustrated that my thoughts were not coming true, I was disappointed at every turn. Maybe deep down I knew it was all a load of bullshit. I had not any answers I cannot even remember what they were asking me. It was just a load of fuss. I wanted to be free away from them. I spent, my time in my room where I could be with my friends. What friends? Deep down I was a very lonely person craving for love, respect and some success.

One day we were having a meal in a restaurant and I said to my father that I was returning to Cambridge, he told me I was not, and that is when reality hit. My life down there was over. "But what about all my friends?" I said. He replied that I did not have any friends. What did he know? Yes I do I replied I have loads.

1998

I got up bright and early and dressed in Benetton clothing, an olive military style skirt, red jumper and long black boots, I was fresh from the shower and I made my way to the kitchen where I made marmite on toast. I was just about to enjoy it when my mother informed me there were some people here to see me in the drawing room. I took my toast in enthusiastically only to be less enthusiastic when I entered, sat in the chesterfield suite was the psychiatrist Dr Red whom I didn't trust, My GP who I had hated since being a little girl and a fat blonde haired woman who turned out to be a social worker.

They asked me various questions and I answered with indifference. I was objective and obnoxious and acted with authority and superiority, whilst eating my toast. Then they all looked at each other and said I would have to spend some time in hospital, and then they left. The social worker stayed behind to instruct an ambulance, I was really scared, why the fuck had my parents done this; I hated them even more than I already did. It came as well, I did not truly believe it would, I was used to a world that did not happen and now the ambulance people were ringing the doorbell. I ran upstairs to my room and shut the door. They came in trying to talk to me nicely. I made for the window and got halfway out of it, I think I would have jumped if the ambulance man had not saved me. The woman began to negotiate with me trying to placate me by saying how nice my art was that was hanging on the wall. I moved further out of the window and then the ambulance man grabbed me and dragged me down to the floor.

Then they picked me up and carried me downstairs. I bit them and scratched them until they had to drop me. My father was crying and said "Don't take her away" and I snarled back at him "I'm the sultan of Brunei's daughter" He sobbed and the ambulance men put the handcuffs on me and dragged me to the awaiting vehicle. The handcuffs hurt like hell; I have never experienced pain like it, the hard steel cutting into your wrist bones. I felt a sigh of relief once I had got into the ambulance because I thought I was being driven to London. At last, they had come for me and were secretly taking me to Piers Windsor and M15. I was so relieved and happy and was just wondering how long it would take to get to London when it turned off at Northallerton on the Al. I sobbed and asked the man and woman to please remove my handcuffs, they duly did and smiled. I then asked them if they had a can of lager or if we could stop at the pub, to that I got no reply.

The mental wing of the hospital reminded me of a Japanese building. To me that meant the Japanese navy was watching over me. They dropped me off and took me upstairs into a hotel like place. Everything was white, new and fresh. I was led into a private room with a sink unit in it, and a bed and a side table and chair. I looked around the room wanting a breath of fresh air but when I went to the window, I found to my dismay it was barred. Where the hell was I? I lay on the bed there was a feeling of calm and not the angst that was in our house. A nurse was sat with me I wondered what for. She just sat saying and doing nothing, she wasn't even wearing a uniform, who the hell was she? I thought.

My parents suddenly arrived and brought an overnight bag with them for me, hastily packed there was barely anything in it. Then Dr Red came in and started talking, I do not remember anything apart from being very scared and him saying I would be here twenty-eight days, it seemed like eternity. I think he also said something about an injection because as soon as he had gone a nurse came in and injected me and then I began to feel very drowsy and I don't know how long I was out for or how restful it was. I seemed to have very vivid dreams. I could not wake up and then I slept then I awoke and then I drowsed, I was drowsy and weirdly unable to do anything. I was fighting it but... I could not. I remember my parents coming in one day and I was painting the three men in black who had taken my body away in Cambridge. I do not know where the paints had come from or why I was painting. I did not speak to them much. After painting, I was tired again and fell back into a confused sleep. Then I awoke and demanded chocolate, they brought me chocolate and I gauged myself and then fell back into a confused sleep.

There was a nurse by my side all the time I did not understand why. Once the nurse on duty gave me some magazines. I am a complete magazine junkie but I could not read them they were of no interest to me, I could not concentrate. I felt ill. I awoke and wanted to go to the toilet, the nurse said she would have to come with me. There was no way I was going to the toilet with someone there and I told her so, so I was allowed to go alone with her stood at the shut door. I did not know where I was or what I was doing. I was not even thinking. I was just semi existing. I eventually came around and felt a little better the first thing I wanted was a cigarette. The nurse led me up the white neat corridor to the end room, a tiny little smoking den no bigger than eight foot by eight foot.

I could not walk. I had been on high heel shoes permanently for two years and combined with the injection of medicine my feet had cramp. I was shoeless as I hobbled along the corridor to the smoking room. The nurse let me in to the tiny den. Sat in the chairs on either side of the room were four witches. The most beautiful of the witches spoke. "Here she is." She was called Lara and was very tall and Jewish looking; she looked worldly wise and street savvy. Seemingly, in years to come I would find out that her boyfriend had drugged her daily with LSD so much that she had gone insane. She was very good looking and seemed all there. Then there were three other ugly witches who grunted a lot and smoked like chimneys on their lamberts and butlers. They were all schizophrenics seemingly, I did not know what that meant, but I nodded duly. I do not think I said a lot, but I remember thinking I was now being watched by the Dutch intelligence. I became very good friends with Lara and we spent a lot of time together throughout my stay. There were other patients too who I spent time with one was a manic-depressive who had tried to blow his head off with a shotgun; I played monopoly with him a lot. Some patients were very unfriendly and violent; twice I nearly was beaten by a man woman for slamming my door too hard. One other patient hit me for no apparent reason.

Mental hospitals are no joke they can be very dangerous places, intimidating and crazy. The staff are not always around to protect you either. I do not know what anybody thought of me in there I am not sure I gave it a seconds thought nor do I now, but it is not really the place you make friends for life because it is a very unstable place. I remember seeing one elderly lady receiving flowers and chocolates every time her relatives visited, she was the only one. I wished someone would bring me something nice apart from Marlboro lights. If I had been a patient with leukaemia or heart problems I would have had sympathy but my mind had gone wrong and that was shameful and repulsive, especially as I had caused it through reckless drug taking. The sorry and pitiful thing is my father had always warned us of the dangers of drugs; we had grown up scared of them.

I had grown up with the images of Zammo in Grange hill addicted to heroin. I had always had nightmares about drug dealers standing at the school gated forcing me to take drugs. Although there were some patients I would make friends with there were a lot I did not ever see or did not want to talk to. There were a lot of very elderly patients, which always broke my heart as to why they were there. They were so frail and helpless. Then there were the weirdoes that you would see drinking cider on a bench in a park or in a subway. One weirdo was reading the dictionary daily, instinctively one knows to stay well clear, and that is not because of the smell.

The very scary thing about mental hospitals is that they are unisex. There is no divide between the sex's bedrooms and their living space. Due to one of the criteria's and symptoms of mania and mental illness being that people have accelerated sex drives I feel that there should be a divide between the sexes, and I felt very vulnerable being amongst males who had lost their minds. The nurses in the mental hospital seemed to be very nice. Most were temporary workers, who came, and went, they did not need to have any sympathy but they were nice. Then there were the full time staff, there was a nurse who was on the late shift and seeing as how I did not sleep, I spent a lot of time with her. She just listened to mad ramblings whilst knitting.

Another member of staff reminded me of Rolf Harris and was actually Australian. One nurse also reminded me of a friend I had once in Switzerland and every time I took my medicine from her I wanted to be back in the place where I had been so happy, never again would I be free like I had been free there and so excited. There was a really nasty man who I dreaded, he did not look nasty but he was evil. Members of staff like him should be working in prisons not mental hospitals. He hated me and I loathed him. He looked a bit like Tom Hanks only much slimmer and he had not a trace of Tom Hank's lovely personality. I dreaded him. There was a lady who was in charge of the refectory and she seemed very nice. She never got very close and just did her job, I liked her until about five years later I was working in a supermarket in Richmond for a promotions job and she walked in and remembered me and looked at me like a piece of shit, and cowered hoping I didn't recognize her. Then there were the staff who tried to talk, but I could not talk to anyone about my information because it was top secret plus.

I think deep down I must have known it was all illusionary and that people would think I was mental. One nurse tried to cajole me and become my friend but I did not tell her anything she wanted to know about my time in Switzerland and my past, which was none of her business. Then one Sunday night a really strange woman came to talk to me. I remember her questions being really funny, and remember I was not very with it at this time so I cannot remember what they were, but I was freaked by her and them. I clammed up and she did not get any answers. She was eerie. I never saw her again.

The worst of my actions was that when you end up in a mental hospital you could summon a solicitor to get you out and fight an appeal for you. I summoned a solicitor to get me out and I also told him my parents had been abusing me because I had been hit several times. I think the whole situation was sorted out by my mother because I had lost interest in the end about living even. The staff tend to be just there and rather like teachers, people you do not tell things to. I thought my whole stay in the place was rather like boarding school, I had friends and people to talk to.

From the first meeting with Lara we clicked. As I got better and over the injections, I was moved into an adjacent room to Lara. The room was en-suite and very nice. It was a little like being in a two star hotel. I had a wardrobe and a chest of drawers in my bedroom and a bath and shower and toilet in the en suite. The maids cleaned the room every morning, fresh shampoo and toiletries were given and if you needed anything that you did not have it was fetched. Lara practiced white magic, which works in parallel with black magic. That was really weird that we were both experiencing the same spiritual feelings and made my belief in the occult even more moored and realistic. It made me go off and practice voodoo with some sticks I had gathered in the garden. I do not really know what I was doing but I was sure I was doing something. Lara and I seemed to gel together, and we took cigarette breaks and meals with each other. We also painted in unison.

She was painting all the mythical creatures like the dragon that we believed in and I was painting the wizard and the werewolf, Piers and other fantasy people. Some of our artwork was actually quite good and we displayed it on the walls and had an art gallery. Lara seemed as offbeat and as set a drift at sea as me, although she was in and out of the mental unit on a regular basis. She was eight years older than I was and had three children; however, I do not think she had custody of them due to her illness. One night we were quite manic and we got some permanent paints and graffittied the window in the smoking room. It was really good fun, it also happened to take the staff three days to clean it off Lara was savvy and told me I must take chlorprozamine I don't know why, but I asked for it and I was given it just like that, no one studied me or asked me why I wanted it, I was just given it, which seems very malpractice. Lara was I noticed permanently all over the boys who were on the ward and was very flirtatious, compared to me I had lost all interest in sex and the opposite sex. As our friendship progressed, it then regressed just as quickly. Lara accused me of staining her suede jacket; I had never even worn it. I decided to leave her alone as she was quite scary when she was mad.

People in mental hospitals are not on an even keel so you can never really make any firm friends, and the friends you do make are a suspension in time. I found I was better off alone and kept myself to myself Lara was not the type of person I would mix with in the real world, I later found out she had a very dodgy past.

Basically, in a mental hospital, there is a routine and the day plans itself for you. In the mornings, we had breakfast, and then we would sit in the lounge and listen to music. Tea break time was usually spent outside having a cigarette and then it would be lunch. After lunch, there were activities such as pottery, theatre or cooking I chose to stay upstairs and paint or sleep seeing how I did not sleep at night. The evening meal was followed by a game of pool or listening to music. Then we would watch a film or television or socialize in the smoking room. The food was pretty good too you could choose from a menu what you wanted.

My mind was not with it for a long time in the hospital. At first I thought there were snakes under my bed and wild animals crawling over me. I could feel Piers around me all the time and I had a bath with him in the evenings. Piers and I were planning our children together. We were going to have six, three girls and three boys. Pier's was talking to the doctors about my recovery, because he had organized for me to stay here for a while. The werewolf also visited and was in uproar because everybody had been locked up in the mental hospital. One night I was in talks with the Caribbean government the air seemed thick and black. I could hear the drums of the deep black magic down there. I was Solitaire out of live and let live. I had all sorts of weird thoughts and I would love to know what had driven my brain into conjuring them up.

It seemed to race from one thought to another. I believed the doctors were watching us through spy cameras. I believed the other patients were witches and other things. Black magic was still my central theme and I was part of the magic circle. I also saw a hallucination of a soldier every time I went down stairs; he was stood dressed in green holding a machine gun. I had all sorts of racing thoughts deeply weird and visual but of course, none was true adding to my frustration. Towards the end of my stay, the hallucinations and thoughts disappeared just as they had done the year previously. What had happened to me why had such an alien force taken over my brain. I put it down to the drugs I had taken and never admitted I was mental or had a condition that was so very serious.

When you are high and experiencing mania, you are a threat to the normal people and a threat to yourself because it is not actually the real you who is doing anything it is this demon force that has taken over your brain. If I had any other illness apart from terminal ones I would be complacent but with it being mental means I can never rest. I am constantly wondering whether I will get through tomorrow all right.

I was not sectioned and had something like five days to go within the unit but I was bored. One morning I had breakfast, eggs, bread and bacon it was delicious. I had not eaten properly in ages; I did not gain a pound. I needed to escape I fled down the hospital corridors in a brisk walk, not looking at anybody, head down as I twisted and turned through the busy medical environment. I found a side door and I was out into the fresh February day. The sun was shining and the first traces of spring had appeared. This was the first time I had been out in two months nearly apart from the hospital garden. I walked hastily away from the hospital not looking over my shoulder. I crossed the busy main road that led away from the hospital and I found a side cut down through some shops to the high street. It was nine o'clock in the morning and it was nice to wander along the high street window-shopping. I made my way to the Victorian arcade and stood staring into a jewellery shop. I imagined the ring Piers would buy me for an engagement and wedding. I stood there for ages just browsing the window and imagining.

I went into Benetton, which had just opened, I wished I had money. I had nothing not a penny nor a visa card. It suddenly struck me I needed money fast. With money I could escape or go to the pub for the day. And then I remembered that the grant office for North Yorkshire was in Northallerton so I walked the long walk to the council offices. I had only been here last July so I knew where it was. I would still have a grant I thought to myself because I was going back to university in Cambridge. I walked in and told them who I was and that I would come to pick up this term's grant cheque. The lady who served me was very nice. She was thin and pretty. She spent sometime on the computer, but came back with a negative response saying there was no cheque for me and it had been cancelled. I disagreed and started to make an argument. A man came through, saw the situation, and then disappeared into the back. I eventually broke down in tears; I was crying and speaking nonsense. I was angry I wanted money.

The nice lady took me in her arms and was comforting me when all of a sudden a policeman burst in and dragged me outside to the waiting police car. Once again I thought I was being taken to London and I had been saved but to my annoyance I was dropped at the mental unit. During the ride in the police car, I had asked the officer if he knew what the magic circle was, and he had replied yes he did. I kept on talking about the magic circle and he was agreeing. As soon as I was dropped back at the hospital, I was marched upstairs and into a room. A foreign scary looking doctor came in, said I was being sectioned for six months, and read me my rights. I kept on screaming about the magic circle and talking about every one in it. They took me away and gave me an injection. I awoke days later cursing myself for what I had done. I faced six months in here and I had brought it upon myself I felt desolated.

I did some stupid things when I had mania but the next thing I did was the most stupid of all. My parents had tried their best not to tell anyone about my illness and when I was ill my mum kept me away from my friends so they didn't find out, but in a moment of madness and loneliness I decided to phone some friends. I had met a boy who came in every day for treatment he was an outpatient and he made me laugh. I asked him if he would get me a bottle of vodka, he said he would and brought it in for me the next day. I took it up to my room and hid it in a coat pocket. I had learnt to hide things in secret places at boarding school. I gathered cartons of orange at meal times to mix with the vodka. That night I mixed myself a nice vodka and orange. The first sip of that liquid was delicious and my body tingled as it had used to. As I drank more, I wanted to talk on the telephone to my friends. So firstly I rang June. I asked her to bring me a bottle of vodka in. She was a bit shocked when I told her where I was. I said I was drying out from alcohol and drug addiction. She then rang my mother to find out what was happening.

My mother was livid I had rung her, I do not know what my mother said to her but I have never spoken to June again and she has never contacted me. I lost a very good friend or maybe she was not. Then I rung Ben, I cannot remember what I said to him but he came up to see me and visited me twice. I did not really have anything to say to him nor was I feeling very well when he came. I had been very frustrated and started to throw things at the wall. I wanted to get out of that place. I tore up a magazine and threw a coffee cup across the dining hall. They injected me and I was out for days, just because of frustration. Ben turned up when I was still drugged up and I was not able to say or do anything. I also phoned Alice that night too and told her I was in rehab for drug and alcohol problems. It sounded cooler than a mental unit did. All in all everybody now knew as people talk and gossip, even your best friends. Rumours spread and before I knew it, no one would ever contact me again. I was a certified loony.

People always say to me that my friends who have deserted me were not really good friends anyway. Nevertheless, it still does not help when you are cast adrift with no friends in the world all because your mind plays tricks on you. I know I should not but I sometimes hope some of my ex friends have some problem one day and they reach out and everyone ignores them. The worst thing about my self-inflicted six months further stay was that it was my birthday in the June and I kept crying about the fact I would be in the mental unit for it. I was most concerned about my life passing by being imprisoned. It was the end of February and I was still manically high. One morning, shortly after I had been sectioned I found my way out of the hospital again. It was nice to wander among normal people in the high street and do every day window-shopping. I had enough cash to buy a four pack and I took it back to the ward to drink in private. The normal routine of the hospital went on and I gradually got better. Coming down off a high is very disorientating, suddenly your brain is back to where it has always been and coping with the reality is very depressing. My mum had visited daily since I had been in the unit but it was only now I was acknowledging her again. My parents and my brother had got in the way of my hopes and dreams; I had resented them and seen them as a hurdle and interference.

However, I realized my mother had stood by me where as some families alienate themselves from the victims of mental illness. Being normal and down on planet earth can be quite a boring existence within the mental unit and as I grew out of telling Dr Red I was Marilyn Monroe's daughter at ward rounds they began to see I was better. I was embarrassed about the way I had acted and knew I could never return to this state, I would never touch drugs again in my life and I swore that. I had lost interest in painting and life in general, but the hardest thing that I could not do was read and I loved reading. I would pick up a book but I could not concentrate enough to read it, nor was I interested. I think I smoked a lot and slept a lot towards the end of my stay, I was quite depressed and ashamed of myself. To me my whole life was over I may as well have served a prison sentence for a crime because I felt lower than low. I felt like I was in the pit of society and I did not know how I would ever pull myself out of it either.

The hardest thing I find to handle about my mental illness is that it is built around an occult a discourse or reality of our dimension in time. People actually believe in it and practice it, it came to me naturally I did not chase it and I sometimes wonder if I should talk to someone about it but I never have. I have never talked to any of my psychiatrists properly I cannot. I have never told them that a completely spiritual manta of black magic takes over me. I just clam up and go silent making them think I have some personality disorder. I suppose it is my problem and it is my inability to talk that has led them to never really getting a proper diagnosis.

I was discharged in April officially earlier than I should have been, but then there is no point in keeping a well person in hospital. Yes, I had been in hospital, something had gone wrong with the workings of my brain, and it does not make me an alien, somebody who you need to cross the street to avoid. It was the first time I had seen my father he had never visited me in the hospital apart from on the first day. He was working down in Selby that day so they picked me up on the way. I was really scared about being reunited with them since I had been a nightmare and rude towards them, selfish and ungrateful for all they had done for me. However, it was ok, we chatted on the journey. Dad went to work and we sat in the car, he was about half an hour and my mother and I chatted. After that dad took us for lunch to a pub and we all got on great. It was like old times. It was at that pub lunch though that I got an appetite, and from then on after that prawn sandwich, I could not stop eating. I ate everything in sight and particularly favoured cream and chocolate, bread and anything really. I ate and ate. I did not touch alcohol in fact I was t total for eight months practically. But I ate and ate I was a very lonely person when I came out of hospital. I had no friends to ring or see, I was completely lonesome, a misfit without any outside link to the world around.

Nobody phoned, nobody sent any post and the scariest thing was that nobody would ever again. I think I just slept and watched TV glad to be at home. Some days I went out shopping but I did not exactly have a lot of money being on the dole again. Well I was not on the dole now I was on incapacity benefit, which is sickness pay and slightly more than the dole. However, I did not really need any money I lived at home, and I did not have any interest in anything so therefore I had nothing on which to spend my money. My interest in clothes had gone, I did not need them anyway I was not going anywhere, and besides I was fat. Due to my eating and the medicine which was the cause, I had gained three stone, which on my slender bone structure was a lot. The mental medicine, which acts on your brain, causes the patient the inability to receive the message from the brain to tell you your body it is full, so you keep eating and eating. Because I was fat, I just wanted to cover up and wear baggy clothing. I had gained the weight within three weeks. Towards the end of April we caught the last of the skiing in Morzine, France it was a good family holiday in which I learnt that I did love my family again.

I did a really stupid thing although I have done many of them. I found a tiny bit of cannabis in my hiding place and out of boredom, I decided to smoke it one night. It was the night I gave up drugs completely. The world started spinning and went very peculiar everything was glaring green lights; of course, I was mixing it with my medication, which is not very practical. I just wanted to sleep to get over the experience. It was the next night that I began to cry myself to sleep since having been well I had noticed, and I have never told anybody about this because I am frightened to what actually is wrong with me now, that my brain was making clicking noses. It is as if the brain physically clicks and moves, it had never done it before. Sometimes it can be discomforting most of the time it is just disserting and worrying. I can hear the sound; it is like when a ligament clicks. Strangely enough, it stops completely after a drink. I've self analyzed myself on the internet and I got a result of tinnitus but I don't think it is, I think it's far more serious than that but I have never had the courage to this day to enquire what it is.

I suppose my analysis and diagnosis would be easier if I would talk to the psychiatrists but I cannot. I tried cognitive therapy and talking about the black magic but I only went once. I find it hard to open up and admit there is something wrong with me. I do not also happen to like doctors very much. I am ashamed of myself and therefore cannot really cope with being ill. I completely denied the fact that I was ill and just blamed the drugs. I did believe I would never have been ill if I had not taken drugs. Now on my medial record I was diagnosed as a psychotic patient, I was suffering from psychosis. I had to look it up in the dictionary several times to comprehend it. I went to bed for a month and sometimes wished I would never wake up from this nightmare called life. As my father put it, "Life was meant to go upwards and yours is going downwards." How true that was. He also used cruel words like calling me a weirdo and a wrinkly dink. I did not care much although it hurt. He referred to my time in the mental unit, as "time in the nut house".

I had begun to sort my interest in my dreams. I would close my eyes at night and the whole world seemed to come alight. I began living my life through my dreams. As I closed my eyes, I could see things. It was very spiritual, I could see human beings discussing things, people sat around tables arguing and arranging. I looked forwards to falling asleep and seeing these things going on. I thought I was special being sent messages, although sometimes the dreams were cruel and were against me, plotting against me and other such conspiracies.

From now on, I had to face the fact that I would permanently live with the clicking in my brain, which I had deduced was a reaction with the mental drugs, alcohol and drug abuse I had done. I would also have to face that most of my friends and acquaintances knew about my time in the mental ward because of my telephoning episode that one night. I had also lost complete respect and responsibility from my parents and hurt them very much. I will never be able to mend their broken hearts. I'll never be able to pay them back for all the money they wasted on my education, in fact sometimes in desperate circumstances my mother tells me she just wants to die as a result of what's happened to me, and I answer that I just want to die too, which I do sometimes. Mainly it is against the reaction from society. My mother says she cannot look people in the eyes any more, and she does not want to speak to anyone, but for me nobody talks to me. I see old school friends sometimes and they walk on by as if I had never existed. In fact, nobody stops to talk to me; they either cross the road or ignore me, as if they have stepped in dog shit.

My favourite programme was Ab Fab. I always wanted to be Patsy. She had this fantastic job at a magazine and all she had done to get it was sleep with the editor.

I was determined not to become depressed and shut myself away again like last year; my life was going by fast. Therefore, I applied for some jobs with the temping agencies in Darlington and eventually one came up at Orange, mobile phone call centre. I was still on the medication I had started in January, so I suppose I was a little slower than normal people were. Since my release in April I had to visit my psychiatrist once a week, this was a complete waste of time as I never said anything; I just sat there emotionless, embarrassed and mute. I would become very depressed during this time and I had also gained a remarkable three stone, I was not happy at all. Going into a work place full of eager, committed and normal people perhaps was not the right environment to go into when you have just been released from a mental hospital, especially when you are trying to live your life as a fraud and not admit it, to yourself or anyone.

I was bored, useless and incapable of the work. I just did not get it after four weeks of training. I sat there every day, the lights were on but nobody was home. I was on another planet, not at the orange call centre interested in my new career. To make matters worse it was my 21st birthday on the ninth of that month in June and I was celebrating by taking Ben to Holland with my parents. The trip was a disaster, Ben wanted to know why I had been in a mental hospital and he began to take the piss out of me for it. Our friendship had changed he was distant and thoughtful about me, I was losing another friend. By the Saturday of the weekend I turned mute, my depression was deeper than ever. I swore to diet down to a waif as every time I looked in the mirror I saw a little pretty girl trying to get out from beneath the layer of fat. At Orange I was getting called fatty, and one girl even asked how come I was so large when I didn't eat lunch, the answer was I couldn't afford lunch. I was very depressed by the end of the weekend and never spoke to Ben for a long time afterwards; he had not even had the manners to buy me a present for my 21st. It was beneath Ben now to be friends with me; he never rang me either for a long time. My friends were dropping faster than ever; in fact, they had nearly all gone.

A week after returning from my disastrous 21st trip I was sacked on the Friday afternoon from Orange, something that destroyed my good normal working confidence for life. It was shattering being told I was not up to the job. I did not tell my mum I just told her the agency had booked too many people to work at Orange and they had to let a few of us go. She was upset, but not as shaken as I was. I had known what was coming when I was taken into the little room by our supervisor. I sank into a depressive state and wondered how I was ever going to live again. What was I going to do? Looking back the world was at my feet but my mental state was terrible. The lingering feeling and knowledge that you have no friends is really paralysing. When you have no friends, you cannot go anywhere or enjoy normal things, and if you do them, alone you look like a weirdo.

My trichotillomania returned that summer as I sat up all night reading and slept all day. In the evenings, I would exercise religiously and I was beginning to lose the three stone. I went to France that summer for a quiet holiday, then in the September I went to Italy both with my parents, I was no longer interested in doing anything exciting so I did not care that I was not with friends. I was so emotionally drained and depressed I did not care anymore about anything. By the end of September, I was thin again and it made me want to face the world again, because I knew I had to do something or I was just going to die. I was off my medication now too. I got a waitressing job in Darlington at Duncan Ballantynes hotel. I am very good at waitressing, so I settled in fast, and worked well right up to the Christmas.

It was the beginning of December and I was flicking through a new magazine, which had just been delivered and found an advert in the back saying the magazine was recruiting staff for advertising executives. I applied immediately. I bought a new suit from the designer centre in York, which from then on I would call my lucky suit. I was a nervous wreck before the interview because I really wanted this job. I had always dreamed of working for a magazine and it could not have been better than being based in Darlington. I got the job moreover; I was on cloud nine I was ecstatic, things seemed to be changing. I was well mentally, better than I had been for ages, but did I really think I could forget my past?

1999

The magazine offices were along Priest gate the fleet street of Darlington. Set in a higgledy-piggledy row Sushi magazine resided over a children's clothes shop on the first and 2nd floor. On the first floor was the graphics studio and on the second floor were the editor's office and mine. My editor was sexy-ish with a large ego not to match, looking back now he was quite ugly; however I had not had sex in over two years so to me anything in trousers was beginning to look good. I started every day by painting my nails, applying my make up, and carefully chosen wardrobe. Then I set out to Darlington parked the car and walked to work. It was soon after starting that I realised the job was like hitting your head against a brick wall. The publisher and the editor who seemed to want to be crooks or businessmen, somewhere between the two had jumped on the bandwagon of free magazines that earned their money through advertising. Only the market was flooded with them, plus the pair had no money to pour into it and they were losing interest fast, as they had quickly realised it was not going to work. I worked harder and harder but to no avail, there wasn't a place I hadn't been, a call I hadn't made, a suggestion nor an attempt I hadn't tried. However, there was no business and the editor and publisher knew it. I had started the job in January and by April, it had shut down.

It had been three and half months of work and there was nothing to show for it but a great social life. With the job, I had made very good friends with the editor's best friend Martin, and I started hanging out with him all the time, going out for boozy nights, watching movies and doing things friends do. Unfortunately, he wanted to marry me only he was fat and ginger. I however fancied the editor and on an outwards bound work trip shagged him in every position known to man giving me the name of Sharon stone. With the job had come social engagements and nights out to functions and openings.

I had begun to lust after the editor because I was so depraved of sex and I spent a lot of time with him. He had not really any choice over the matter when it came to shagging me as I made it very clear what I wanted. In the end, I wished it had never happened as he did not want anything to do with me and it was on the last day at the magazine I found out what he really thought of me. I was packing away my stuff ready to leave and I needed to ask him something. I went into his office only to find he was not there but his computer was on. He was writing a screenplay one of the characters listed on the character description page was an over zealous advertising executive with schizophrenia. I screamed, ran into my office grabbed my things and fled. How did he know my guilty little secret, how did the world know my defects? I worked it out that a mutual friend of June and mine who was friends with the editor would have heard it from June and told him. But I did not have schizophrenia I had psychosis, well that is what I had been diagnosed with so far. I must have given all my estranged friends really something to gossip about. I was a social pariah and I knew it.

My mother had been going to see a homeopathic doctor and suggested I go too. I was willing to try anything I'd been free from medication for six months now yet even though I had a life I was still depressed. I asked the homeopath for a cure to the effects of amphetamine and cannabis, as it was these to blame for my mental breakdown.

My dream job had ended, I was a crossroads again. Ben came to see in the April and for the first time in a while we got along as we had done before in the past and I was still good friends with Martin. I had spare time on my hands and filled it through looking for a new job and exercising. A job came up at a pr agency in Darlington, I wore my lucky suit and I got the job. It was an administrator's job for the conservative party pr company.

I began eagerly and really loved the job, some parts of the computer operation were a little hard but generally I was doing all right and within weeks I was promoted to writing press releases in addition, doing photography jobs. I was enjoying it and doing well until........The world started going a little funny I was paranoid and hallucinating. I met Prince Albert in the tearoom at work and he followed me around for the rest of the day. The photocopying machine went wrong and I got the blame for it although it seemed to be operating on its own and was broken. I was sent into town for some stationary and got cast a drift on another planet and disappeared for ages.

Life had gone distorted and it was only later that I realised that it was the effects of the homeopathic tablets I had started to take. That night on the way home, I nearly had a car crash. Everything was trippy I felt like I had taken some hallucinogenic drug. That night in bed, the world was moving. I thought the army had gassed the nation with some sort of gas experiment, and then my demons came to me. I thought my mother had turned into Mara Hyndley and she was going to murder me, I thought my father had turned into Fred West and he too was going to murder me. Everything was rushing, I could not sleep, and I felt awful having really bad nightmares whilst being awake. I was scared and yet I was away on a trip that I could not control.

On the Saturday I ran away, my parents followed me in the car. I got all the way to the gas station in the village where I told the gas attendant that I was going to make a civil arrest against my parents because they were Myra Hyndley and Fred West. The gas attendant looked strangely at me and then I was packed into the back of the Volvo estate and taken home, only at thirty miles an hour I jumped from the back seat out of the car. I thought I was a super hero and could do anything. I just walked from the car unhurt. My father has never since travelled with me in the car again unless the doors are all locked. I was locked in the house, which had come alive to me. Black magic was happening in my bedroom the shadows and the glitter of it all were appearing to me. I was imagining two Egyptian Arab princes were after me; they had appeared in my thoughts before and were part of the black magic circle. I could feel them they were so very close. When I looked out of the window, I saw that summer had come and all the trees suddenly turned into the Seven Wonders of the World. My imaginary grandfather the sultan of Brunei's father had come back to haunt me too. In the evening, my bedroom was alight with black magic.

Everything seemed to have turned to gold and was shimmering in the summer heat. The smoke from my cigarette melted through the dusky air. The reds greens and blacks were highlighted; the air was thick with magic. Two Egyptian princes came into my room and sat with me prompting me to play "killing an Arab" by the Cure on her CD player. Dark shadows were alive in my room and around the house; the black panthers had come alive. Images of princes and snakes were shifting through the room and I resided on the bed and lit a cigarette and felt blessed the black magic had returned to me, it was my only consolation.

I was very manic and now I was sure that all my mythical friends were true, as I had reached this state without the aid of illegal drugs. I was happy it was all true, I knew it had been. It was the summer of the royal wedding between Sophie and Edward; it was also Ascot week when the doctor was called to see me, to whom I spoke gibberish and nonsense. As she had arrived, I had just had my head blown off by a shotgun by the werewolf. The doctor rang my psychiatrist Dr Red and he came out to see me. My mother said she did not want me admitted to hospital and said she would look after me. I was prescribed risperodone and told to rest. How could I rest when this fantastic dream life was back? I was now diagnosed with having affective schizzo disorder. This was my third diagnosis and not my last. I was ill for quite a while, I remember going to Scarborough for the day with my brother, mum, and Piers Windsor. He was back and at night I could hear him in the loft, I thought he was living above me, watching me closely. I always thought I was being watched. I still do.

My mother had phoned the pr company to tell them I was ill, as soon as they found it was a psychological illness I was sacked. Martin came through to see me too. One night I went to his house and drank all his dads' vodka and smoked his cigars, it was after that night that my mum explained to him I was a little psychologically ill. He changed his phone number and I have never seen him since. I also towards the end of my illness had organised to go to Manchester to see Ben. I thought I behaved perfectly all weekend but of course, my mother had told him I was not well, so of course everything I did was regarded as mental. I have never seen Ben either since that weekend.

Once again, I had lost all my friends and social life through my illness. I must do something really terrible when I get ill because I drive everyone away. I know I talk rubbish but I do not deserve to be alienated every time I am ill or do I?

I had nothing, how was I going to pick myself up again after this. I went back to Duncan Ballantynes restaurant and got my old job back waitressing. My shot at a career had been a joke; I was back to where I had started for a while. Until I broke down I couldn't cope anymore with life I just wanted to die, so I rang up and said I wouldn't be back and I went to bed, signed on the sick again and wasted my life away.

I was still quite manic and feeling a little funny from the high dosage of risperodone. I was down on my knees I literally had no friends and no one to turn to; I had lost everyone and everything. I wondered what the hell I was going to do in the future, whether or not I would just live with my parents alone for the rest of my life. I wondered whether I would ever go anywhere ever again, and then out of the blue an invitation came through the post. I never got invitations any more or any post. My mother handed it to me with surprise. The dropout loner had post. It was an invite to a wedding from a girl called Sue.

I had worked with Sue at a pub in Darlington, between me finishing school and going travelling. She was marrying a man in the army at a village not far from where I lived. She had kindly invited my brother too. It was my only social occasion on the calendar and I decided to dress up. I still had some money left over from my last pay cheque from the PR agency and I frittered it away on a £600 suit. I had been looking in Hello the previous week and saw Princess Stephanie of Monaco in this adorable sky blue Chanel suit, it was fitted and showed all her curves. I was in Harrogate with my mother the following week and we were driving down the parade when I shouted "Stop." And there in a boutique window was the exact replica of Princess Stephanie's suit. We parked the car and hurried to the shop. It was a tiny expensive boutique with few and select, original designer clothing. The Joseph Janard Sky blue suit was on sale from £600 to £200 I bought it straight away, it fitted perfectly.

The wedding was lovely, the church service was short, a little 'four weddings, and a funeral' ish and the reception in a marquee on Sue's fathers land was good fun. I had to be careful drinking a lot on my medication but I downed quite a lot of red and white wine and was fine, although I got very tired later on and needed to go home. I met up with Sally who I had also worked in the pub with too and we arranged to have a night out together the next week to catch up again. I had not seen her since January 1997 when I had run away and seeked refuge at her house where I had first experienced the spiritual feelings of black magic.

The following Friday night I got ready to go to Sally's house. She had her own cottage on her father's estate in Richmond. My father warned me before we went out "Don't come home with a squaddie." I am afraid they were words of wisdom. My mother drove me to Sally's, I had lost my license due to having been ill, the psychiatrist informs the DVLA and you are not able to drive for a while. We had a drink of vodka and took the dog for a walk before going out. It was a beautiful July evening and the pubs were spilling out with young couples in love, how I looked at them with envy. There were People in groups going drinking and crowds of friends laughing together, how I missed that. We went for a drink in the Fleece and I bumped into Lara, who seemed to be out on her own drinking. She started talking about something and I was agreeing, but Sally was looking at me as if I was from another planet. Sally did not speak to Lara apart from nodding her head to her. Sally wanted to leave and go to another pub.

She did not ask me how I knew Lara, but she did say, "You don't know her do you? Seemingly her mother was a prostitute." I did not say anything, especially not where I knew Lara from. Sally was a bit funny with me after that, she began looking at me strangely and was distant. After being harassed in the dodgy disco bar we were now in we took a taxi to Catterick and went to the seedy Stacks nightclub. Built in the 70's this nightclub had seen better days, it has since been knocked down. It had the aura of low life military roughness and the decor of a faded cheap tacky pleasure beach place. There were not any good-looking men and the music was unmemorable. We sat drinking on the look out for some men, I was desperate it had been so long I just wanted to be held.

I had just run out of money for another drink when, through bleary eyes, a burst of energy entered the club. It was Tony whom I had met in January 1997 in The Buck one afternoon. He instantly dashed over to me and kissed me full on the lips and hugged me, I hugged him back. Then he bought me a drink and told me he had always wanted to meet me and had thought of me several times since meeting me in the

Buck that afternoon. He thought I was pissed so he asked me to come back to a friend's house for the night. I accepted besides Sally had pulled a young twenty year old and was going to have a party of her own. I fell asleep immediately on the couch at his friend's house and slept until morning. Tony had been checking on me all night. We left straight away and he took me back to Sally's house. It was seven o'clock in the morning and Sally's front door was open. We went in and sat talking on the sofa, then we kissed, and then that good old feeling in my loins ached and I felt the stirrings of lust. We went upstairs and made love, it was quick but satisfying and the unification of us. We left there pretty quickly Sally was not in a good mood nor was she happy at the thought of me having made love in her spare bedroom.

Tony took me for lunch to the Holly hill pub. We ate fish and chips and drank pints of lager. It was a glorious day and it was great to be out again. After getting to know each other better and chatting we went for a long walk along the river and fell asleep in the hazy sunshine. Tony was romancing me he was my Errol Flynn. Tony did look a little like Errol Flynn. He had thick locks of dark blonde curly hair. He was muscular and thin, toned and fit. His huge blue eyes were fluttered with dark eyelashes and he had bow shaped large mouth, at forty-two he looked thirty-eight. He was a bit worn around the eyes but he looked well. He had lived his life well and enjoyed the finer things in life although he could not afford them. For a working class boy he had a class that was distinctive, I put this down to his German mother and military background. Born in 1958 in Cyprus Tony had travelled the world with his father, a sergeant Major in the armed forces as a boy. He had been in and out of schools worldwide and so his schoolwork fell way behind, all he knew was the army life, and so at sixteen it was no great surprise when he signed up. His father had told him that he could not afford art school for him so there was not any other option. He served as green jacket, posted in Ireland and Gibraltar for four years and then he moved to the Royal Engineers where he specialized in diving. He bought his way out of the army at the young age of twenty-six determined to make a life as a deep-sea diver. He travelled the world diving, living an exotic lifestyle and a hedonistic one too. Divers are not averse to drinking neither heavily before working nor to smoking lots of drugs. Combined with the pressure of the sea and an altered mind Tony got the bends, decompression sickness.

The company he worked for sacked him as he was no good anymore to them and he was blacklisted from the registers of diving professionals. He came back to England from America upset and confused. After a drunken night out in Manchester with some friends, there was a drink driving accident and Tony was paralyzed. After spinal fusion, operation and various other procedures and six months in hospital Tony could walk again. He went away from England as soon as possible and went to Germany to live with his mothers relatives. There he became a gangster, equipped with a gun and a stash of cocaine; he was wanted in Germany so he fled to Spain where he married a pretty Senoritta who had his son. Washed up on the beach Tony was bored, jobless and skint and so started doing drug runs in the early 90's from Spain to England. Eventually he gave it up and his marriage also ended. At thirty-eight he was living with his parents in Richmond and working on the roads. The previous week before he met me in the nightclub Tony had been to see a psychic who had told him he was about to meet a girl with whom he would share eight years of his life with. Tony was a lot like me, not only in looks but also in the fact that he denied he had the bends. I only knew because Sally told me, and she knew everything about everybody in Richmond.

Tony made me laugh, he made me smile and he took an interest in me, which nobody else did. I told him from the start I was on medication and I was diagnosed as mental but he did not believe it. The first thing my father did was to tell him of my illness in the hope it would put him off me, but it didn't he arrived daily with military precision to pick me up and take me to the pub somewhere. I must have been to the majority of pubs in the north east on my travels with Tony and eaten in most of them too. He was very generous and paid for everything. I was not even put off him when he referred to himself as an old alcoholic. Going for a drink every night became my life, I had two or three glasses of wine or four or five pints of lager. Unfortunately, the reaction against the medication and alcohol brought me out in acne, which was very unattractive, but Tony did not care, even so though I stopped taking the risperodone. My mother doled them out every night and I threw them away. I noticed he did not have any friends either like me, which brought us closer together as we relied on each other for company. At the beginning the sex was a breath of fresh air something I had neglected because of my illness. Having thought I was godly, I had shunned sex for my mind-blowing made up life of fantasy. Tony was very possessive too and did not allow me to talk to other people; he did not like them knowing his business nor the possibility of losing me. My parents took me to Italy in the September of that year and I had a strange depressive holiday. There I was on a beautiful island, Elba and all I wanted to do was sleep and read. I stayed in the hotel for the entirety of the trip. I also noticed for the first time a distance in people's eyes when they looked at me, wariness and it bewildered me. I had missed Tony and the day of my return to England, I will never forget the look of love and excitement in his eyes as he saw me again. He was dressed in combats and a red t-shirt and he looked splendid as he took me in his arms and swirled me around.

At the end of September, he took me to Torquay on holiday. The jaded seaside resort was dull at the end of the season and the dismal B and B was quite sordid and dirty. We did not do a lot and I found it quite depressing wishing I was not there and a longing to go home to my mum. Tony noticed too and asked me whether I was taking the piss out of him. I was not but I was not sure if we had a future either. Nevertheless, something kept me with him and I was unable to let go, I liked him deep down even though our relationship was weird and he was a father figure and we ended up in a brother sister situation.

In the October Tony decided to buy a house. He said he had been looking for one for ages. He did not want to live in Richmond because he hated the gossip and he was bored with it so we looked in Darlington. Tony wanted a beautiful house or flat in the west end but I do not think he knew the cost of them. We ended up looking for properties around the thirty thousand mark; there was not anything very nice most were ex council houses. Then we were in the estate agents one day and I noticed a little house in the town centre in Beckdale Street it was twenty thousand, what was the point of having a huge mortgage?

I knew from instinct this was the house there was something about it. The narrow hallway had a small ornate Victorian decorated room off it. There were the original cornices and fireplace and a bay window. Then there was a larger back room with the kitchen and bathroom on the extension. Upstairs were two decent sized bedrooms. It needed a lot of work but at least I could put my mark on it. Tony liked it too even though it needed gas central heating and new double-glazing. Tony went through the procedure of getting a mortgage and we bought the house. I think he thought I would move in with him straight away but it was nearly two years until I did. I spent my days now shopping for bits for the house, Decorative items and furnishings, I loved having a house it became my hobby. We decorated the bathroom, the kitchen and eventually the whole house in time. It became a very elegant little place or the cave as we called it. My mother was horrified I was living in Beckdale Street; it was the slums as far as she was concerned, her nose turned up and she shifted in her seat if she ever came by. Number eleven Beckdale Street was a higgledy-piggledy Victorian mismatched street. Built by drunken builders the rooms were all askew. The back yards housed the rats and these shanty buildings were built on the remains of the old back-to-back housing. At the end of the road was the telephone exchange, which we occasionally got letters from telling us of the dangerous emissions it was depositing to nearby residents. At the other end of the street was the west end the rich end of town, where I used to frequent. I soon settled into life on the dole sat in front of the television watching sunset beach, then I would trail the shops for bargains for the house, I think I grew very bitter and twisted being poor. I began to begrudge the rich and wealthy. I was stuck in poverty and was one of those people I had learnt about at school, the poor. I had nothing and the future was not very bright either. My depression was hidden from Tony; I could put on a smile. I liked being left in the house on my own whist he was at work, I quite liked being depressed.

2000

To ease my boredom and the long lonely nights I spent on my own whilst Tony was working nights and days, he suggested I come with him on journeys in the cab. I saw the country, parts I had never been to before. We visited Nottingham one Easter weekend. I looked around the city and then we went out to the pubs and clubs. I went to Manchester and Liverpool, the west coast and other remote locations. It beat the humdrum boredom of being sat at home. I shopped and ate in cafes and waited for Tony to finish work so that we could go to the pub. Going to the pub was a daily routine for Tony and I and it was not just one pub it was two or three different ones. We drank and drank and drank. We egged each other on and drinking became our hobby our interest in life. Quite often, we would discuss the merit and calibre of the lager as if it were wine. We did not much care what type of pub it was either, posh, spit and saw dust or a family type one, working class, middle class or upper class, we could be seen in a champagne bar quite often. We were not just drinking heavily in pubs we were also drinking at home. Eight tins of lager per night was the routine or a bottle of vodka a day at the weekends.

We drank throughout the day and as the years went by our drinking developed into morning drinking too. We woke up with a hangover and cured it by having two or three tins of lager. Saturdays afternoons were spent in the pub pints of lager flowed through our hands. I was almost intolerant to alcohol, after two or three pints, I thought I was sober. When we drank in

Darlington, we visited many different pubs and did a pub-crawl or went through phases as to where we drank regularly. We never made any friends along the long windy path of drunken pleasure. The money we spent on alcohol deprived us from being able to buy decent food, clothes or things for the house, alcohol was number one. Tony even drank and drove. He covered his can with a sock and drank from a black can. I used to go mad with him and told him what would happen to him if he was caught but he did not seem to care. We were a modem day Bonny and Clyde we lived an existential lifestyle. I always think the film a bout de soufflé is reminiscent of our relationship. I became known in the pubs as a moll, no one knew that I was from a wealthy upper middle class background nor did I tell them.

I knew my drinking was out of control but I had nothing to live for I had no future and no friends if I hadn't drunk I would have died from boredom or depression which was temporarily lifted after me taking that first drink.

I was very bored and very skint so I decided to get a job. Tony went with me to the job centre and we found a good job in promotions, which paid good money. It was working for N power swapping customers of other gas and electric boards over to the cheaper brand. It involved standing in Scotch Corner service station for the summer wooing customers. I got the job after several interviews and tests. I started work with enthusiasm and determination to get sales so that my pay packet was good. Moreover, I was good at it I changed twenty people a day which was far higher than the target. I worked with one other girl called Marie, she was older than I was and shier than me and did not enjoy the job but she stuck it out. I was making good money and I could afford nice things again like clothes and makeup. I would have stuck with the job but unfortunately in the August of 2000 it went bankrupt, I had only worked for three months, however I could afford to take us to Cyprus for a holiday at the end of August beginning of September. On my last day of work with Marie, something weird happened. We were threatened by some charvas and Marie broke down crying in shock. She said "God not only am I doing this scummy work and working with someone who has been sectioned but now I'm being threatened." I was shocked that she could be so nasty, and to this day, I would love to know how she knew I had been sectioned. It was as if I had some contagious disease, but I knew it would distance people from me for the rest of my life. In addition, my dirty little secret was public knowledge.

I would never see my friend Marie again; we did not keep in contact. Cyprus was brilliant; it was one holiday I will never forget. We went on holiday subject to placement on arrival and found out it was Larnaca where we were staying. We were the only people going there and we were solely dropped off at the Kasnipolsky hotel all on our own. Nothing changed there then for us. We wandered around for a bit after having unpacked and found we were opposite a lovely five star hotel. We immediately ended up in it's outside bar by the swimming pool.

We visited Limassol and Ayai Napia, saw and shook hands with Jeremy Healy one night at the Castle club, sunbathed on Nissii beach and ate scrumptious food. We even made some friends who were called Liarris and Paul, she was from Latvia and was very pretty and he was from the USA and was very rich.

They actually wanted to know us and we spent a lot of time with them for a couple of days. Paul thought I was a supermodel. It was nice to socialize with good people. I bought jewellery and clothes. I got chatted up over a hundred times by nice men making me feel very worthy and superior, I was in good shape due to my heavy workout plan and diet I had done before going, and my clothes were funky and attractive. We also drank a lot, and on one occasion with the Cypriote mafia. I was experiencing bad nightmares about the army at night but luckily it did not effect the holiday and I was happier than I had been in a long time. On the final day, we were at the bar in the five star hotel, when a group of gangster-ish looking men with strong cockney accents arrived and offered to buy us a drink. Some of the men looked like club bouncers, heavies and some were businessmen. They said they worked for Bruce Springsteen. I do not know whether they did or not but they had notes and schedules and lyrics of his which they showed us. They wanted me to come on tour with them. I think I was just going to be groupie or one of the businessmen's bit on the side, but they were very forceful in persuading me to join up with them and tour the world. I stayed well clear not really believing that they had anything to do with Bruce Springsteen. It was a bit of a rush still. I was still glamorous and attractive to strangers and people who had not heard rumours about me.

We had drunk our way through a £1000 worth of alcohol on this holiday, I think it was time to start facing the situation I had a problem yet I still drank a bottle of ouzo before boarding the plane, my alcohol problem was out of control but I didn't want to stop. I had done a very stupid thing to whilst abroad I had mixed valium with vodka on several nights to get a high. Christ I was using prescriptive drugs very much in the worst way possible, I enjoyed the sensation although it had repercussions when I returned I was set a drift on a depression that led my trichotillomania to get worse and I felt devastated and bewildered. I also experienced hallucinations when I got back to England, they were Egyptian ones, and I was seeing the sphinx, the pyramids and jewels, lots of them. They disappeared and I got back on track. Going forwards was what I had learnt to do. It had been a great summer and a special holiday. I had not had a good time like that in years, it sealed Tony's and mine companionship and clinging, superficial love. Tony had had the time of his life too; it had been nice to see him happy. We could not stop talking about the amazing time we had had and bored people silly with our tales. We even planned to go and live out there one day, Cyprus had given two very weary and lonely people a lot of love and encouragement for the future. We felt like we both had destiny and promise for our existence again.

When I got back to normal, again I noticed Teesside University was wanting applicants, I thought why not maybe I am ready to study. Studying and living at home meant I would not be tempted to do anything foolish and I would be able to get help from my mum with my work. I lived in Darlington with Tony now most of the time but still went back to my mums occasionally, and Middlesbrough was not far for me to travel to every day in the car. I chose a BA in media studies. I had always wanted to be a journalist so it seemed the right course and I enrolled and started late September. I enjoyed it very much; it was my kind of thing at last! I made friends at uni, coped with the course, and passed the first semester.

It was Christmas 2000 and my parents asked whether Tony and I would like to go on the annual ski trip. We accepted and my parents paid for an apartment and the flights for us. Tony had skied in the army so we were both looking forwards to it. The holiday passed but I found I had to take my risperodone; I was having manic and depressive thoughts. I thought the people in Morzine were against me and I was having huge doubts about the future of my life, I was going nowhere with Tony and it hung heavy on my mind. My dreams were very vivid and I was drinking an awful lot. However, I found I could keep my mania under control this time and not let it get the better of me, I did not tell anyone either. We skied and some days when it was raining we hit the bars. It was a strange holiday, nothing really happened, and I decided ski trips were more work than relaxation. I found it very hectic and fast paced. I was glad to get home.

2001

It was around the time of foot and mouth 2001 when I began to be heavily depressed, I was in a two up two down, I had no money again due to a tight budget of a student loan and I did not have much hope for the future even with a degree, who was going to employ a mental patient. My boyfriend was a loser, a road digger, I was at the bottom of society and it played on my mind. I began to drink bottles of white German wine and the world went funny. I thought everybody was a witch and I was very high, although again I tried to control it. Tony thought it would be best for me to go back to mum and dads for a bit until I got well. My mother took me to the psychiatrists and they prescribed me sulpiride. It hurt me, it made my face numb, I cannot properly describe the feeling but it was like high pressure in my brain and nose, everything felt constricted and tight. It was very painful but it brought me down. In the time I was high I had been allowed to go back to uni and start the new semester, however I got all my work together that had to be done for the term and did it all in a week, whilst Piers Windsor was communicating to me from a submarine. He was back in my life. Our relationship was one big love story and we were so in love. The romance and the thrill I felt was unreachable in reality.

Tony and I had booked a four-day holiday in Amsterdam before Easter; I had to get well to be allowed to go, so I had a target either snap out of the mania or do not go to Amsterdam and I managed, the new drug brought me back quickly to planet earth.

It was a dark night in February; I dressed in a new black suede gilet I had bought the previous week in TK Maxx and a tight pair of Miss Sixty jeans. I brushed my long blonde hair and applied my make up carefully. I was only going to the Tavern, the biker bar in Darlington but I liked to look good. Rain was falling as we crossed the busy main road to the pub, the red lamps of the dark interior in the pub and the beating rock music lit the street, and we entered the pub and sat at the bar. People always eye you up when you go into the Tavern. It is a dark seedy pub full of drug dealers, alcoholics, hells angels and scum. Tony spoke to a boy sat behind us seemingly he knew him from Richmond. We ordered our beers and sat staring at the optics; well Tony was staring at the optics my attention was now focused on a very beautiful man, who had his back to me. He was shouting and raving in a right temper to the landlady about the current effects of foot and mouth. He looked like landed gentry.

He was wearing a tweed suit had had a beautiful posh English accent, very clipped with a hint of the West Country. He was six foot four, wide shouldered and long legged, with a mass of thick black hair. He became my new obsession. I had a thunderbolt, and fell in love instantly; I had to hold this man. I got down off my stool and walked past him to the toilets as I passed him I took my hair out of it's ponytail and shook it. When I came back from the toilet where I had touched up my makeup, he was sat with the boy behind Tony. Our eyes met. He looked me up and down with interest, there was shock in his eyes, and he fell silent. I got back up on my stool. We finished our drinks and left, I had one more look at him before leaving. Moreover, from that day on there was not another day that I did not think about him. Not one night when my body did not long for him, that my groin did not ache and that I dreamt to be with him for the rest of my life. After that, I never went to the Tavern pub without looking immaculate, I had to see this stranger again and find out everything there was to know about him. I never saw him again for a long time, but I was sure I could feel his spirit around me. It was hard trying to enjoy Amsterdam when I had met a man I wanted a relationship with.

We visited museums, ate drank and drank, shopped and had an excellent time again. Getting away from England seemed to relax us both. It was as though our position in society was affecting both of us and stressing us out. Being unknown and free spirited in a different country pleased us and made us happy. In four days, our alcohol bill was £600 respectively. Something weird happened to me though I was experiencing delusions of black magic, shadows were appearing to me and I was having anxiety attacks. I took my medicine and it calmed me. I was in control though, and when I saw a blue magic van, I knew that is what had happened. Blue magic stops black magic and white magic from reoccurring. Piers was also following me insane with jealousy that I was with Tony. The alcohol had made me delirious, but still I could not stop drinking.

I was recovering as I finished my second term at university, and then I came down to earth with a bump of depression as the long and empty summer stretched in front of me. I started to look for work and found a job with the Northern Echo newspaper working in Promotions. Basically, I had to stand in a busy shopping centre somewhere in the northeast of England, sell the paper, and give away free samples of products with it. It was very easy work and very boring. We were trying to get people to subscribe to the dying paper but no one was interested. The job took me all over the place and it was nice to get out and about and meet people. The pay was not very good but I managed to save enough to buy a holiday to Rhodes in the August for two weeks.

The poverty-stricken streets were getting me down. The people in the street liked to sit outside on the pavement and drink all day in the summer. They downed cheap cider and fizzy white wine. Most of them were crack and heroin addicts and they were pretty grotty. I got talking to them one day and found out they had nicknamed me Barbie because of my clothes and hair. They invited me around a couple of times and I found out about their poverty-stricken life. One family who had four kids would send the kids out on a Sunday night to steal the charity shop deliveries so that they could clothe themselves. They had the four children living in one room on mattresses; there were no sheets of comfort. They lived in squalor and ate food from Netto.

I did not mix with them much as we were completely on a different wavelength; they just reminded me of the poverty-stricken state I was in, going nowhere fast. I had finished work one day and was wearing horrible black trousers, a polo shirt, my hair was in cotters and tied scruffily back, and I had minimum make up on. I took Tony up to the Tavern for a drink in the afternoon July sun. We walked into the dead bar and were told by the barmaid everyone was outside in the beer garden. I pushed open the beer garden door and there sat at the table was my beautiful stranger. I walked right up to him, sat down opposite him, and asked where he was from. It was very unlike me but I had had this man on my brain for nearly five months and I had to know who and what he was about. He was from Gloucester. He seemed very angry again and did not seem to want to chat. I began talking about our holiday and for some reason I asked him if he had been to Morocco, he said he had, I wanted to go there with him and bask in the sunshine touching his body. It was apparent he didn't want to talk, the situation was awkward enough with Tony being there, if he hadn't have been I would have kissed the stranger. I sat very sexily and finished my drink, and then we left. I remember feeling satisfied that I had found out something about the mystery stranger.

The Northern Echo job was getting very boring and the pay wasn't as good as selling windows so I moved on to work for a double glazing company, the bonuses were large. All was going well and I was quite happy until Tony started working very late nights and I was left alone I couldn't sleep and started hearing voices very badly when I was trying to get to sleep. They were very disturbing and very frightening. This was the first time I had experienced this trauma. I found that if I lay under the covers they would go away. They were nasty and saying cruel things about me and my life and my past. Sometimes they were people I had known sometimes it was Piers Windsor. Sometimes I wondered whether it was radio waves being emitted from the telephone exchange that was causing them. It only happened at night when I was alone. It was that summer I was certain that Eleven Beckdale Street was haunted with an evil spirit. I was a very disturbed person who wondered what was happening to me. I was nervous wreck and sought solitude and medication in alcohol. Life continued as normally as it could be and we decorated the front room that summer. I did it with the thought of my stranger in mind. I did not tell anybody about the voices. I would now live with hearing voices constantly everyday until March 2006 when a new medicine Abilify was recommended to me...

It was holiday time August 2001, I was really excited. We began the holiday celebrations in Newcastle airport where we downed several pints of lager. Then we had a few drinks on the plane. Then Tony erupted and started going mad, calling me a slag and accusing me of all manner of things that I had not done and said. Then he went for a cigarette in the toilets and got caught, and then a woman behind us had a go at him for being out of control, so he had a go back at her and called her a slag. We were questioned when we arrived and it was only my diplomacy that stopped us from being arrested, I said we had had a domestic row. The pilot said he did not know whether we would be allowed back on the flight on the way home and we were let off. A police car took us to collect our luggage. I thought I was in a James Bond film and was being given special treatment. We arrived at our hotel to find out that it was not very nice, by this time the world was going a bit psycodelic for me. I do not remember much about the next few days, but I remember clips.

At one point, I was hallucinating in my bed and I was out with the Sultan of Brunei's father again, then my Russian father, the prince turned up and he was controlling me. I know we were drinking heavily and I took my clothes off in a café during a thunderstorm, but then it all went blank and I lost about two days of the holiday and woke up in a clinic. Tony was with me and told me what had happened, I did not want to know. I had got very drunk and smashed a television screen in a pub resulting in £400 worth of damages. I had also snogged an English guy and Tony had knocked me out with his fist after I had slagged him off and broken my cheekbone. All I could remember was sitting in a café saying loudly and "who the fuck do they think they are?" I was embarrassed and feeling unwell. I took my sulpiride and hoped I would be fine. My mother was ready to fly over and all sorts, but I came round, sort of, although I was still hallucinating and having funny thoughts. The rest of the holiday was not all that fun although we made the best of it. Falaraki was not really our style so most nights were spent on the balcony. It was on this holiday that we started taking a lot of photographs of me. It turned out that a lot of them came out really well, but people started to think I was a model as we went all over the place photographing me.

Tony was a good photographer as well as an artist and sculptor. The holiday was a nightmare really especially when I had to go to the police station to get my passport back and pay the money. Thankfully, I got the money back on my insurance. We were allowed on the flight but were not allowed alcohol and had to sit in a special place. I was very upset by having ruined the holiday I had looked forwards to it all summer. Tony swore he would never go on holiday with me again. My parents were mad with me too; my mother was really, upset and had worried herself to death. I now accepted that travelling did not agree with me anymore.

We had cut back a bit on alcohol ever since I was ill during the holiday, but I still drank in small quantities. Tony watched what I drank but even so we'd still managed to spend nearly £500 on drinks. It did not stop when we got home either we drank and drank some more. I felt very ashamed of myself for having gone mental but I still loved the high. I loved meeting my imaginary friends and feeling like I did, and the scariest part is I can't control it, it just suddenly happens to me and I go along with it really believing in it. Tony was now beginning to doubt his first thoughts that there was nothing wrong with me, he was facing up to the fact I was mad and yet I still could not admit it to myself. I blamed drugs for my downfall and believed if I had been allowed to come down from them I would not be mental, I now blamed alcohol for my problems.

The first time we went to The Tavern when we got back was a late summer night, inside the pub was dark and stood at the back, eyes glittering like a Christmas tree was the stranger, my obsession. He looked me up and down, I must say I looked good, I was wearing my tight miss sixty jeans and studded high heel mules and a leather flying jacket. In a booming voice, he bellowed across the pub "Now that's what I call a woman." He flushed. Then he made his way surely across the bar and shook Tony's hand." How are you my friend?" He said in his aristocratic voice. Tony replied. Then the stranger made a comment about why do women have to wear nail varnish and makeup and looked at me very hornily. He then told anybody that was listening that he was going to the next pub along the road and left. My heart sunk, he was very handsome that night. Seeing him fuelled my dreams.

I went back to university at the end of September and to my delight found that we were studying writing for the broadcast media, which involved writing a film script. I already had my screenplay in my head before the professor had finished explaining the module. It was about the stranger, Tony and me, the first three times I had met him, and in the end, Tony prostitutes me to him to escape poverty. I felt as lowly and as desperate as a whore did in real life. I got a high and a buzz from writing the screenplay, and when it was finished, I could not stop reading it over and over again, it was good and

I handed it in at the end of term with glee, desperately awaiting the result. I attained a high mark in the eighties, after the script had been sent off to check for plagiarism as my professor did not believe I could write anything so good!

During Autumn I visited the Tavern regularly and it seemed every time I went there the stranger was there. The stranger and I started to look at each other in a secret manner. He would always be sitting in the window of the pub visible from the outside. As I approached, he could see me and I him, we then looked through the side window at each other and held the gaze or gaup for about ten seconds. I was dumb with love for him; I could not say a word to him.

In November, Tony started working night shifts for long stretches, leaving me alone in the house for long periods. Since I had no friends no one came to see me and I sat alone with a drink and the television. I had plenty of time to think about the stranger, I tossed and turned at night and longed for him. One Monday night I began going to the gym at the local sports centre, it only cost a £1 to get in. I was working out and all the lads decided I looked like Ursula Andres in the Bond film Dr No; it was a nice compliment seeing as how she is my favourite movie star. Then I met an old friend I had not seen in years, Jim. He came over to chat it was nice to see a friendly face, I found out he only lived around the corner from Tony and I, and we had never bumped into each other. He asked me out for a drink. I thought why not he is an old friend, Tony will never find out and maybe just maybe I might meet the stranger. I went to Weatherspoons with Jim, who is a bit of an alcoholic and we got really pissed, had a really good laugh and arranged to meet the night after. We met up Tuesday and Wednesday, Thursday and Friday. Friday night is a big night out in Darlington and the Weather spoons was very busy. Jim and I were in the corner when Bri turned up. Bri was a drug dealer who drank in the Tavern and knew the Stranger so I asked Bri about him.

Seemingly, he was a farmer, I had guessed that. He organized a music festival like Glastonbury.... Moreover, he was married to a woman who was nowt flash. My heart hurt and my jaw dropped. Of course he was married that is why he never made a move on me, it all fitted into place now. I was upset and kept thinking he cannot be I love him. I drank to ease the pain and blot him out of my memory. I went home with Jim that night and unfortunately slept with him, it wasn't passionate, remarkable or memorable it was pretty awful really. And then the worst thing happened in the morning I was getting dressed and about to go and say goodbye to Jim when he came in the room and handed me a wad of cash. I snatched it out of his hand, tore it in half, then threw it up in the air, and ran from the flat. He had been a friend of mine long ago. Now he thought I was a prostitute and he had seduced me. I ran around the corner back to Tony's house and showered trying to scrub away my guilt. I felt terrible and suddenly realized I loved Tony. He came in an hour later from work, I took him to bed and made love to him, I did not want to lose him. The shame and guilt was riddling me and I realized I was lucky to have Tony, and suddenly I did not want anything else.

That was November; it was the beginning of December when I decided I needed something which would fill my days. Something to give love to and receive it back unconditionally, most of my life I had been giving sex to receive love and it somehow never worked out. Therefore, I began looking for a dog; of course, I was told how ridiculous this want was, and that I would not be able to look after one. I even went to the dog home, but the process of obtaining a dog was too long winded for me. In early December, I met an old friend briefly who was pregnant, she was blooming with happiness, and it was then that the idea of a child once again struck me as a good idea. We had tried in Cyprus and in Rhodes to no avail, but this Christmas we would get lucky. Tony finished work before Christmas and our party season began in earnest. Our drinking had not curtailed in fact it was increasing now to a crate of Stella Artois a day and regular frequent visits to the pub. It was over this Christmas period that I had a realization that I had to stop drinking. We were in a pub in Darlington and someone said we looked like ghosts. I went to the toilets and looked at my crinkled face aged prematurely with excess of alcohol. I had to stop drinking, and in fact, I did because I was pregnant.

2002

I had no morning sickness but I missed my period and I felt different. I was snapping at Tony and feeling very tired all the time. I was late in going to the doctors because I was in shock that I was pregnant, and I suddenly was not very sure whether or not I wanted to go ahead with the pregnancy or abort it. However, of course I could not abort it I had asked for it to be brought into the world. I went to the doctors and proceeded in the pregnancy. Fortunately, for my baby I had never taken my medicine so there was no way it could have harmed the foetus. I had a busy pregnancy. Tony took sick with white finger and cried one morning before work begging not to have to go. I rang in sick for him and from that day, he never went back. The strain and long hours had taken their toll on him and he needed a rest, so with a baby on its way it was up to me to earn what we needed for the baby and go to university. In January, I started work at the local restaurant. I was having a really good time until I was five months pregnant and I was showing slightly. My boobs had grown so large they shadowed the bump making it hard to decipher whether or not I was pregnant.

The restaurant owner who would not want to pay maternity leave got very funny indeed and sacked me through a phone call made by his head waiter, saying I was no longer wanted. I felt that sickly feeling you get when you have been sacked, it encompasses your body and makes you wobble. Tony got a gun from the cupboard and went round to the restaurant. I really thought he was going to use it but seemingly, he chickened out when he got round there and just stood at the window watching them inside. The world cup was on whilst I was pregnant through the long hot lazy summer. I broke from university in the May, I had not told anyone there I was pregnant, in fact I had not told anyone I was pregnant I did not have anybody to tell. At five months, I told my shocked parents who at first were not very pleased, but my mother came round after a while and helped me out as much as she could. As far as the pregnancy was going, I was well I was strong and fit, I ate well and I was happy-ish. Practically tee total I felt refreshed but watching Tony daily drink himself into oblivion was distressing especially when it began at seven o clock in the morning. I had a hard pregnancy on my emotions and cried myself to sleep at night. Money was tight but we managed to decorate the house in arrival for our son. However, I had also brought more shame on the family with having had an illegitimate baby.

We had decided to call the baby Domini. I knew everything there was to know about pregnancy I read and reread the NHS pregnancy book very night before bed, the only subject I missed was the giving birth section. At night as well as crying myself to sleep, I had terrible leg cramps and towards the end I had pains down the front of my thighs which were executable. I was not tired and I had the odd Guinness for iron for the baby, besides it relaxed me in the evenings. I dreaded the blood tests and the check ups but they were ok really. I was just scared of doctors; I did not trust them at all. I had seen the midwives faces too as they read my notes and saw I was a mental patient with schizzo affective disorder, they became hard and distant, a little spooked and remote from me.

At eight months, I was doing a lot of walking still through the back streets of Darlington mainly. I was still out at the pub on Friday nights and was still enjoying myself. People couldn't tell I was pregnant because my 36 double G's were bigger than my bump, so I got away with people thinking Id' just put on a little weight. Only someone in the Tavern had realized I was pregnant. It was the stranger, Rory to my dismay had walked in one night, he had stood in the doorway larger than life in his leathers his shoulders were huge, he filled the entire doorway. He commented "you've put on weight; you're not pregnant are you." I did not answer I cringed and wished I was not. Another person commented behind my back "she'll be a single mother with a mental problem." How did they know I was a mental patient? I sat and meditated that night trying to figure out how they knew my secrets, had Tony told them. I asked him and he said no then I realized I had met the white witch Lara in that pub one night and she would have told that man, because I remember she was talking to him. Great so now everyone in the pub knew I was mental. It was about at seven months when I started going paranoid. Not badly but bad enough. I was having nightmarish and odd thoughts about people, and believed they were all against me. Everybody was against me; they were talking about me and plotting to kill me or trying to make me into a prostitute. I was not chronic though.

However, Piers Windsor was now living in the house with me.

At eight months, I had my show early in the morning and then I had contractions because I was only eight months though I thought it was just some bad pains and suffered the pain in bed all day. I asked Tony for a strong beer and he gave me a few cans I thought it would take the pain away, it did not they got worse and worse. Tony was crying because he thought I was going to die. He had drunk fourteen tins of Stella that day and could not drive so I had to phone my, mother to take me to the hospital, which was in Northallerton because my mother had wanted Domini to be born in Yorkshire not County Durham. Tony was completely drunk as at eleven o clock in the evening at the hospital, he packed me into a wheel chair and drunkenly slammed me down the corridor to the maternity wing, banging me off walls haphazardly. I was screaming, I was in so much pain I could not move. They put me straight into a bed and gave me gas. I screamed and screamed more and more. It was like one of those horror stories of pregnancy in a film when the woman dies. My mother and Tony were expecting me to die they said later. Then the medical staff said I was not in labour so they gave me a drug to stop the contractions but I puked it up all over the nurse. Then they gave me something to bring on labour, and more gas, and more gas until I had emptied the bottle and I was still screaming. The drugs did nothing I was immune to them. A big fat nurse burled into the room and shouted at me to stop this nonsense I couldn't I was in so much pain, she said I was ruining other women's births because of the screaming. Then a patronizing cow came in and asked me if it was because of my mental problem that I was screaming. I was screaming because I was not dilated and the baby wanted to come out and I was in serious pain not because I go mad every now and again. I told her she was a stupid bitch. Eventually a doctor came in and gave me an epidural and I relaxed, then as time went by the pain eased and then midwives came back in and said I was going to give birth soon. After a few pushes little Domini was born. He was whizzed straight away into the special care unit where he stayed for four weeks.

The relief after giving birth was incredible I lay on the bed in calm and the pain had gone. The nurse who had asked me if I was screaming because I was mentally ill once again patronizingly said to me "look at you just staring into space". I was just so relieved it was over and was having a moment to myself.

I could not sleep and was having paranoid thoughts. Therefore, the hospital staff gave me very strong paracetamol, which did not help. I did not sleep for five nights and was very ill because of it. I could not concentrate and I was not interested in baby Domini. I asked my mother if I could go home with her, she agreed it would be best and I discharged myself, I had a bad spell of mania during my first night at home. I believed the radio was talking about me and that I was ugly and would never have beautiful looks again. My mother was shoving sulpiride down my neck like smarties. I could not sleep. In the morning I remember being depressed and anxious about the new baby, but I could not do anything. We wanted to move Domini through to Darlington to the special care unit there as Northallerton was along way from home. Before I left Northallerton, a psychiatrist came to talk to me. He was young and thought he was clever. He wanted me to tell him my story from the beginning. I closed up on him there was no chance he was hearing anything about me. My mother told him I was fine and we left Northallerton hospital, who then turned around and said Darlington, would have to care for my psychiatric issues as well, because I now officially lived there. They did not care; I had never opened up to them or asked them for help so they had no feelings or sympathy for me.

Domini was in special care for four weeks, which was a long time and also gave me chance to return to my old ways of getting pissed. I did and loved it. I was feeling a little fat after the pregnancy and decided to take Adios to rid of my baby weight.

When Domini did come home, I was on my own. Tony did not care for the baby and it showed if he cried he put him in another room. He refused to contribute any money towards Domini or I and I had to rely on benefits. Tony was working nights and I could not cope. I did not have a clue how to care for a baby. I had never even touched a baby before in my life and I was scared. Then I went psychotic. I could hear voices everywhere throughout the house, snakes and rats were all over me. I celebrated yon Kippur and went all spiritual. I was playing loud music and singing I was happy. My parents had Domini for the weekend and I partied with Tony. We drank and drank, I stayed up all night on Saturday night singing Madonna songs, and then I cannot remember anything apart from shouting at Tony and being nasty. His interfering parents came round and phoned a doctor, who brought a social worker with them, and then they sectioned me for six months.

I began to cry hard I could not believe I was sectioned again, what had I done? I walked peacefully into the ambulance with Tony and was driven away in the late summer sun of September 2002 to Darlington psychiatric ward known grimly as P1. I was taken into a cold room with a cold doctor who asked me questions, I answered with awkwardness and nastiness. I was then put in a room on my own I remember watching the boy opposite me exercising. It was peaceful and nicely decorated in the ward, but then I was moved downstairs because I was not from the right area to be on the nice relaxing ward. The downstairs ward was grimy and horrid, dirty and cold. There was one nice television room for women only but it was always empty and the television room, which was mixed, was full of boring and ill people. Then there was the grotty smoker's room where I resided. All was well I was playing cards for days with one boy and then they gave me some drugs and I went madder. I began taking off my clothes and dancing in front of the rest of the patients. I was taken to my room.

This part is hazy but I remember telling a nasty member of staff that she was wasting food and she should think of the poor and starving in Africa and the next minute I was bundled down to the secure locked ward downstairs. It was awful, I was locked up. It was cold and reminiscent of prison. The other patients were edgy and dangerous or high, but I was high too. All I wanted to do was sing and dance. I nearly snogged a young boy too, but I was not really interested in that. In some ways I was quite happy being back in the mental hospital, I enjoyed socializing and I had many friends inside, which I did not on the outside. Nobody visited me apart from my father; I did not have any friends anyway and Tony came too and was shocked that I had ended up down there in the secure ward. I think I was down there for three weeks I remember asking how long I would be in the hospital, nobody ever told me, but I had been diagnosed with bipolar disorder this time. The new consultant did not bother to read any of my old medical notes. Everyday I remember looking at photos of Domini and crying. How was I ever going to be able to cope with looking after him? I was moved back up to the grotty ward and out of the secure unit. I socialized a little but I mainly went to bed and slept, and slept. The nurses were very angry that all I did was sleep. I remember laying in bed on Bonfire night tears streaming down my face. I wanted to be free and at home. Tony kept sneaking in cans of lager for me, which made every day a little more bearable. I took baths and became a recluse inside. I did not eat much the food was disgusting; I ate double deckers from the machine. By November, I was well again but they would not release me although I was going home regularly. I was now on quetiapine. The main thing I checked upon was that I could drink with the drug. Which wasn't an ideal question seeing how I was a new mother.

I could not just be discharged normally because I was now a mother, and it was completely different from just fending for your self, so the hospital suggested I go with Domini to a mother and child unit in Morpeth, Northumberland, very far from home and very horrid. It was supposed to be lovely seeing how it had been opened by Lady someone but I will bet she did not spend time in it. We were locked in and it was boring and grotty. I survived two weeks before I said I had had enough. I said I was willing to go back to Darlington P1 and Domini go home to my mothers again. I was well and although it helped me adjust to a new life with Domini, it was a waste of time. I felt even less human after my time there, the doctors looked down their noses at you, yet the nurses were fare. My consultant discharged me; I was unsure how he managed this task considering that throughout our meeting he just stared at my tits, never blinking. The only good thing to come out of going to Morpeth was that I met a girl called Claire who lived around the corner from me in Darlington. She had psychosis however; we got on very well together and promised to stay in touch.

2003

I was home and I fell into life with Domini perfectly, it was easy, well not easy but easier than before when it had seemed so hard and impossible. We weren't a conventional family, I do not think I was drinking any less either. Domini slept through the night so I did not have to worry about getting up. He was bottle fed so I was not breast-feeding. I stopped taking my tablet it was interfering with my drinking and making me feel funny. I was not mentally ill though. I still had not faced up to being a mental patient. Even when I heard someone in a pub one day say under their breath, she's a loony isn't she. I hung out with Clare a lot she had become a good friend and she was not mental either. She was my new best friend. We were from completely different backgrounds but our illnesses had both been triggered by drugs so we had something in common. Clare had been brought up in children's homes and had really seen a different life to me. She was plagued by social services and CPNs, I was not luckily my social worker visited three times and then left for Australia.

A new one came but I said I did not need any help unless they were going to send a cleaning lady around to help me. My CPN visited regularly every week in fact, it was good it kept me in step and made sure that I had to stay well. I thought of my CPN as a friend, which is something you should never do. During the next six months I was a dedicated mother looking after Domini solidly, and scared senseless social services would turn up again My mother took us out a lot and Tony worked, it was a quiet time and nothing much happened. I was well without medication and happy too. I saw the man of my dreams once he ignored Tony and me, but he looked incredible. After that, Tony went to the pub one day alone and met him.

He gave Tony an invitation to come up to his music festival in June. Tony gave me the invitation but said we would not be going. I hid the invite in my knickers drawer; I now had his telephone number.

One night when Tony was out at work I text messaged Rory saying, "You are lucky I am not coming to your party or I would have fucked the living daylights out of you." I did not care anymore whether Rory was married or not, nor about Tony, I wanted Rory and that was that. I turned my phone off in case Rory replied and Tony checked the message. I did not get a reply. I kept asking myself why, why has he not replied, and then I was sure, the telephone number was wrong and he had changed it. It was the night before my birthday in early June. The town was starting to get hot. Tony and I had been rowing frequently over him accusing me of seeing somebody else. Well I was in my dreams but not in reality. One night he practically pulled the whole of my hair from my head. However, this particular night before my birthday we went to my parents for a BBQ.

My father ignored Tony as usual which I think angered Tony and fuelled his temper. Tony drank quite a lot and I had to drive home. We had had a good day we had stripped the woodchip paper from the bedroom walls ready to redecorate. We rowed about my fathers attitude on the car journey home but then when we reached home I put the house key in the door but knocked it with the baby car seat I had in my hands. The key broke off in the lock and was jammed meaning we would have to call a locksmith. Tony went literally mad and started kicking the shit out of me and fisting me in front of a little crying Domini. He said he could not remember doing it in the morning but he seemed compos mentis. He kicked me again until I took refuge in Domini's room. Tony's parents turned up and called a locksmith, they tried to talk to me but I had had enough of them too. When they had gone, Tony came into Domini's room and I asked him to leave shutting the door on him so he kicked it down on top of Domini and me. I was scared for my life as Tony smashed the bedroom and all the pictures of me up. I lay awake that night planning my departure. It was early in the morning I went down stairs and entered the bathroom. Tony was in the shower, shoving a vibrator up his back passage in a thrusting manner. I was shocked and said excuse me and left. I ran upstairs and went back to bed sobbing did this mean he was gay too. I waited until he had gone to work, the disgust repulsed me. I packed my things and rang my mother she came around instantly and we left. I ignored Tony's phone calls and text messages.

I went back to live with my mother and father. This had been a tough decision to make as I had no friends and no life back at the little village. I settled back into life at home, it was hard on occasions having been used to my own way of doing things and freedom. I arranged to pick my belongings up from Tony's house, which was quite an emotional night as a slanging match between families arose, and it was not very pleasant.

It was the middle of a hot summer, having left the back streets of Darlington for Mum and dads house in the country. I felt free for the first time in four years, another nightmare had ended. Mum decided to buy me a flat in Darlington in the posh west end. It was a maisonette on a lovely private estate. I dreamt of the interior design plans I had for it day and night. It was now just a matter of time before I moved in waiting for the mortgage paperwork to go through. It was also a tremendous help having the grandparents to help with Domini.

I knew Rory had had a party because I had been invited to it, so I decided to try to find his telephone number on the internet since I was sure the number listed on the flyer was incorrect. I do not know why I had had that intuition but I was right. I typed his name in the search engine time and time again using different variations of subject matter and eventually his name and number came up on a gig listings website and sure enough, there was a new number. I anxiously yet eagerly re-texted the message "It's a good job I didn't come to your party or I would have fucked the living daylights out of you."

I waited and waited and a day later, a text arrived. I could not read it and waited a whole hour before opening it. It read "I'm still recovering, but that managed to raise a smile." I smiled and texted back, "I'll raise more than a bloody smile." The texting went on for ages, he wanted to know who I was, but I remained incognito to keep my mystique. I ended up telling jokes or saying what I was going to do to him when I got my hands on him. He invited me to the pub for a drink but I replied I had nothing to wear.

In between my days with Rory and sex-texting, I spent my time with Claire and her son. We entertained the children or went shopping. My other time was spent shopping with my mum. Claire could not believe what I was doing but egged me on even giving me a text to send, "I'm like a martini anywhere, anytime any place."

I do not know why but I got a tinge of a feeling of the aura of black magic, I did not go mental but I decided to look it up on the Internet and find out some information on it. I found a very high profile website that was all to do with mind control and the CIA. It was very similar to what had happened to me and led me to start thinking about conspiracy theories. It is a very interesting website and can be found under black magic. At this time I hadn't taken my quetiapine since Christmas, partly because I didn't want to gain weight, and I hated taking treatment because in my eyes I wasn't mentally ill still. In my eyes, I was ill because of the effects of drugs and I would never be able to face up to the fact that I had long-term brain damage and needed to take a pill. However, the worst thing of all I would start to take the Adios pills again because I wanted to be very thin to go to London.

I planned to go to London to see Hannah whom I had not seen in a long time and spend the weekend with her in Wandsworth. I took the bus from Darlington, which was long and hot, and I was stuck next to an awkward teenager who had the social skills of an ant and buried himself in his Ipod. Arriving in London always gives me a buzz and I felt alive and young again. Hannah was on great form and we got on together as well as ever. On the Friday night, Hannah had booked a table in Soho at Leslie Ash's new restaurant. It was Moroccan inspired and we ate and drank well. After that, we ended up in a rough old bar in deep Soho. Here we sank two bottles of wine. Just as we were finishing off the world was starting to go wonky on me and I went to the toilets stumbling. When I returned Hannah was nowhere to be found, she had left. Suddenly I was out in the fresh humid air of Soho at night, swaying drunkenly through the streets looking for Hannah. I was scared; I could see triple of everything and lurid men were eyeing me. I dashed for a taxi and gave him Hannah's address. Arriving back in Wandsworth the taxi driver demanded £30, which I did not have. I had to give him my address and promise to send him a cheque, I only just got away with it as he was threatening to take me to the police station. I puked up everywhere that night in the bathroom and just as I was cleaning up the mess at five o clock in the morning Hannah came in. She did not know where she had been. She said she did not even remember leaving me, but worst of all she had been doing this time after time every time she went out. She thinks she just wanders the streets for hours. Lately she has been waking up in police station cells.

On Saturday, we shopped in Covent Garden, Knightsbridge and Regent Street. I shopped like never before buying Domini wonderful enchanting presents. I found special boutiques in Covent Garden where the dresses were unique. The Saturday night was spent meeting Kathleen another old school friend in Fulham and we dined at the Terence Conran restaurant. It was fun catching up. Although Kathleen made one comment, that I would end up in a mental institution because I had been complaining about the price of utility bills and how I could find alternative solutions. I do not know whether it was a dig at me or a hint. I resigned to the fact that everybody knew I had been sectioned, although I did not talk about it all weekend. On Sunday after having a quick look in Liberty's it was time for me to go home. I was jealous of my friends and the lives they had, and it sent me into a slight depression. There they were with the world at their feet living it up in London, and I was in the grim old north with a baby branded with the title single mum. On the journey back I texted Rory I am about to have my clit pierced. It was days later that he told me to fuck off.

I arrived back in dreary Darlington and my mother and Domini picked me up. I do not know when things started going wrong but it was soon after I had arrived back. Life started to be a little trippy. I began having vivid dreams, Emilio Pucci contacted me in one dream so I started to paint Pucci inspired prints on pieces of wood, which filled my days. Then I heard voices seemingly Piers Windsor was watching me from Thailand. I was out of it quite seriously, but with having the aid of a CPN my mother rang her instantly. She brought round some tablets and told me to go to bed. I did and I was even worse, I was hallucinating in my sleep and having nightmares. The murderers were coming to get me and rats were in my bed.

On the last night I spent at home, I was manic about Tony and what had become of him. I was looking at photos of him and imagining all sorts of nasty things. I thought he had been killed; I was very distressed about him. The next day my parents took me to see my psychiatrist in Darlington hospital, he and my CPN sat there whilst I cried about Tony, I was wittering on and on about him. I suppose I had spent four years of my life with somebody who was no longer around and I was having a nervous breakdown. They decided I should go to a residential unit in the west end of Darlington. It was a bit weird arriving there as I had worked in the same house when I was thirteen for my duke of Edinburgh's award when it had been an old people's home. It had completely changed now but it was still strange being somewhere I had been before, especially in the circumstances. My parents left me and I sat in the grand gardens of the Georgian mansion for ages smoking. I was actually manic thinking my parents were in a horror movie scenario. In fact, they were deeply upset that I should be ill again. I was called into the weird mental unit to write down all my possessions on a sheet of paper, at which point I thought I was Princess Diana reincarnated. I then got bored and left the unit to go to the petrol station to get some cigarettes.

When I returned it was teatime. I had noticed that all the staff were very odd and cold. They did not seem to care; it almost felt like a prison. At dinner I sat with two weird men, everybody in the unit was seriously mental and disfigured it was beginning to scare me. One woman looked like my old housemistress at school in Scotland and I really believed it was Butz and was very scared indeed but glad she had ended up in here. As the evening went on the weirdo, man I had been sat with at dinner offered me a drink. I accepted thinking it would be vodka and tonic but it was just juice, however I firmly believed it was alcohol and got quite merry anyway, and entertained him with my manic talk. As the night went on I smoked more and more, later on I went to bed but I couldn't sleep I was imagining Jack the Ripper had turned into Prince Andrew and he was haunting the corridors. I went for a look around the unit and found some weird old rooms with funny medical furniture in it. The whole place was beginning to spook me out and I decided in the morning I was leaving first thing. I went into the lounge around three am in the morning, a Thai man was on duty I sat down next to him and demanded he get me some lager so that I could get to sleep. I pestered him for a long time, but the cold uncaring man said nothing, I went away in a mood, if I could have had a drink, I would have been able to clear my head and sleep. It was a really awful night in the unit I do not think I slept a wink I just wandered around the house believing I was being watched. At some time during the night I had a shower and believed I was in Dr no, the James Bond film and that Piers Windsor was coming to see me very soon.

I had a hearty breakfast in the morning served by weird staff. The unit was as if I were in a horror film filled with zombies and other species. Then I went to my room closed the door and locked it. The room was similar to a cheap motel one, I climbed out of the window and walked calmly down the drive, no one was following. As soon as I was away, I began to run twisting and turning through the roads of Darlington that I knew so well. I now believed the whole of the unit had been murdered throughout the night. I could see the bloodbath that had taken place and as I walked through the town, I was waiting expectantly for the ambulances and police to be blazing through town with their sirens sounding. As I reached the centre of town I saw Ballantynes hotel where I used to work I decided to call in for breakfast. Something stopped me from ordering a brandy; I did at least have some sense left. I ate a full continental breakfast in the plush hotel. The staff were eyeing me up and down with that look in their eyes, they knew something was wrong with me; I was probably talking to myself. I went to the cellars to go to the toilet and I met Piers Windsor, I had met him here before. I could see his shadow in the mirror and the haze of his cigarette. If only I could meet Piers my turmoil would be over, I thought. I paid the bill and continued my walk into town. I really did not know what I was going to do I had no one to meet and nowhere to go. I thought I would buy something to drink, then go and sit in the park, if only I had done that.

I wandered around House of Fraser department store and bought some nice Miss Sixty shoes in the sale. Then learning that the pubs were shut I went to Marks and Spencer and bought some lager and some cocktails in the can. I then went to New Look and sat in the changing room drinking the cocktails. I was asked to leave the store. I hazily retreated and wandered up the town to Weatherspoons pub. I ordered a pint of lager and bought some cigarettes. Then the world went a blank. I remember meeting two boys and I remember emptying my Marks and Spencer lager into my pint glass but that's all..........That was around eleven o clock some time later in the afternoon I was in a car with five men they dropped me at Tony's house and let me in with a key. It was very weird how did they have a key. Who were they? I shut the door of the little semi, I felt like I was home but I was not the house had changed, there was an oddness and emptiness, a depressive linger in the air. It was bare without the lavish decoration I had stripped it of. Nobody was home, at first, I lay upstairs on the bed stripping myself of clothing, and then I awoke and moved downstairs to the settee. I awoke again from a nightmare and I knew I had to get out of that house. Not thinking in any rational manner, apart from trying to escape the voices in my head, I ran half-naked through the town until I joined the main road out. I was running very fast, with energy and stamina. I was dodging cars and running from one side of the road to the other like a lunatic.

Eventually I hopped across a fence into the golf course and streaked across it. I saw someone on their mobile phone who must have been phoning the police because the next minute I was hiding in a bush and the next I was being bundled into a police car. They gave me some overalls to put on, I do not know whether I was naked or semi clothed but I knew I had lost my new shoes. It was my first time in a prison cell. I was shoved into a cold dungeon. It was awful, there was a bench, a shower that did not work and the rest was just cold stone. I lay on the bench motionless for a while. I do not know how long I was in there but I do know I began to hit my head against the wall hard, it seemed to relieve the pain of being me. A police officer kept checking on me from a slit in the door and I kept demanding a cigarette. That was all I wanted a cigarette. Eventually I was let out and I had a shower. They gave me my clothes wherever they had come from, and I put them on. There was a social worker there for me but I had nothing to say to her or anybody. I was bundled into a plush cop car and taken to the mental unit P1 at Darlington.

Once here I was taken into a room by a nurse I knew from my last stay and I was read my rights. I was being sectioned, for how long I do not know but I remember vaguely it being six months and the feeling of terror swept over me. I was put in an en-suite room and the first thing I did was to light a cigarette. I was quite manic and pissed off I was here again. I do not remember the first night of my stay.

The first memory of my third stay in a mental unit was that I had decided to go to the shop to get some lager. I had just sneaked out of the ward and down the steps of the building, when I saw my parents coming. They saw me too and began to shout at me telling me to get back in. What happened next was awful. I ran back into the unit and onto my ward. Then I ran into the smoking room and hid behind and young Arab guy who was in there. My parents who are not allowed in the smoking room were being told to go away by the nurse and leave me alone. They were demanding to see me and I was hiding. I would not go out and talk to them. It was a bit of a show, but when I get ill, I seem to have no pride or shame. They went away and I relaxed and came out of hiding. As my mania resided I began to go to the smoking room a lot more. I knew some of the patients from before so it was like catching up with old friends. Because it was the summer holidays, there were a lot of university students in who had obviously been overdoing it on drugs. All of a sudden, I was having fun with the crowd who were in, and I was causing trouble with one girl called Lizzie, who I did not like. The smoking room became divided I and another girl who could not stand Lizzie either took to being very bitchy. I fancied the Arab guy too and had a fling with him stealing his attention from Lizzie. Having a secret fling in the ward was a bit hard, as we had to keep away from the watch the nurses so a lot of time was spent sneaking behind couches in the television rooms. It did not last long maybe a few days, he was very confused and I am not sure if he was well enough for a fling. We started sneaking bottles of vodka in, and I started sneaking beer in. Life was not too bad apart from a blazing hot summer was happening and I was in a prison-esque place. That is the thing about being sectioned you are more or less in prison. Claire came to see me once or twice but I think it was a painful reminder for her being back on the ward. Worst of all I had missed Domini's 1st birthday, it was lucky he came to see me and that I had bought all his presents before I became ill. I felt sick with guilt that day.

It did not take long and I was completely normal again, by the time I had a social life on the ward all other thoughts had gone. I was well within two weeks or less. Some new guys came onto the ward who were trying to recover from alcoholism, they were serious card players and I joined them playing poker and other games late into the night, it was great fun. The best I had had in a long time. Within three weeks, I was going home on days and coming back at night to stay in the unit. I also spent a lot of time sleeping because the medicine made me groggy. There were talks with the psychiatrist to allow me to go back to university at the start of term to finish my course. It was hell that I had become ill again, near the start or university; it was heaven that they allowed me to return so that I did not waste another year of my life. Therefore, I had to take it easy until term started and stay every night in the unit. Every time I am ill I lose something this time I nearly lost going back to university for a second time and I lost moving into my flat that my parents had bought me because they couldn't trust that I would take my pill and look after Domini responsibly on my own, since they had found my stash of pills that I had not taken. My flat was put on the market, I had lost complete independence.

I was in hospital when my grandmother took ill. She came to Darlington too. I visited her twice a day as I was there too and sat by her bedside. She was seriously ill. It brought me round her being ill, because I had to be well to look after her and my mother. Due to her being ill, I was let out of hospital just after a month. There was not much point in me being in there as I was completely sane. I started back at university in late September and grandma died.

It was good to be home. University had started and I had one aim and that was to finish the year. Life was very strange after losing grandma, having lived with us for ten years we had been very close .Something very important happened just after the funeral of my grandmother. I had a consultation at the hospital, because my psychiatrist had taken a new posting, I had to meet my new one. The psychiatrist was a woman, Russian and not very nice. She disagreed with the medication quetiapine that I was on and said, I should be on lithium. Lithium is the cheapest drug there is to issue this is why it is given out randomly. A full-scale argument between my mother and her broke out. My mother had always fought to keep me off Lithium. Then my mother broke down, I thought they were going to have to get her a bed there too in the unit. She was crying from the heart probably releasing her grieving too. She was saying how she cannot cope anymore with me getting ill. It was very embarrassing and awakening and I vowed at that meeting that I would take my tablets no matter what so that I never became ill again. I also faced up to the fact that there was something wrong with me and I had now to conquer it instead of giving into it. My mania may have been a feeling that I enjoyed but its repercussions are just too serious and affect too many people's lives.

After the realization and the funeral, I was driving down North road in Darlington one day when I saw Rory in the window of the Tavern. He looked surreal something I would never be able to have, he was gorgeous. I began to text Rory again talking about his spirit and comparing it to a mistral. Whatever! He began texting back, at first, he was quite hostile but by the end, he came around and really wanted to meet me. One night at Claire's, I lost all my inhibitions, anxieties and fear so I decided to arrange to meet him. He was overjoyed and said he had not been on a blind date for years. So we fixed a date for the Friday night, eight o'clock at the Tap and Spile in Darlington. I sat all day terrified on the Friday in the student's union bar at university, texting Rory. We were both scared, and excited.

I went to Claire's to get ready that evening in mid November. She said I looked like Princess Diana when I was ready. I had bought a new cream jumper dress for the evening and I wore my Russian inspired coat. Shaking with nerves I gave myself some Dutch courage in the form of three cans of lager and some vodka, not a lot of alcohol in the scale of things, however....I'd been waiting for this moment for years, I'd strategically seduced him by text and then...... I walked through the back streets of Darlington to get to The Tap and Spile pub in the centre of town; it was a cold, cold night. I paused as I entered the pub there he was at the back, as handsome as ever. He sat bolt upright mesmerised when I walked in. He leapt to his feet when I reached him and asked me what I wanted to drink. I sat down and waited, when he returned and put the drink down he began to talk but.... My world began to sway, then I felt that feeling, and I could not believe it I was sick over him..... He picked me up and carried me back to his friend's house. I passed out besides him on the bed. At about three am I awoke, Rory was awake. He recalled to me what had happened. I was so embarrassed, I wanted to crawl under the carpet and die. I raided his friend's fridge and nicked some beer. I needed it to rid me of the shame. After three cans of John Smiths we had a pleasant conversation and learnt all about each other, talking and talking. He seemed immune to what had happened and I made him swear he would not tell anybody. We got up at about ten am we had not made love, we had kissed and hugged. The conversation had been interesting. He walked me back to Claire's house holding my hand. My worst fear now was that I would lose him just as soon as I would found him. He was going to see his sons that afternoon but promised to meet me later at the pub in my village. I waited all day anxious that he would not call and sick to the bone about the happenings of the previous night. What a disaster!

Rory rang that night and I met him in the village pub. All the locals were admiring his dragster motorbike. I went on and on about how sorry I was about puking over him. I would not say it was a really successful night but he wanted to see me again. I think he was a little uncomfortable about dating a woman to whom he was old enough to be her father but he relaxed a little towards the end of the night. We kissed goodbye and arranged that I would go to Stanhope in Weardale the next weekend. It seemed along way away. We texted each other all week as usual, I went to university looked after Domini and shopped.

It was a dark Friday night as I set off on the long road to Stanhope. I had never been there before and only just knew the way. The night was black and I had trouble seeing. Rory rang me because I was late; he thought I was not coming. But ten minutes later, I met him in the Packhorse in Stanhope. Both of us were very nervous, several Guinness's and lagers later we were slightly more relaxed. After we had chatted for a while, he led the way home on his motorbike and I followed in my car. We were going up in to the mountains and then down a very dark track. At the end of the track was a large Georgian farmhouse with several ramshackle outbuildings. It was a large place set in sixty acres of land. I could smell game birds as I entered the house. It was very dark and damp; obviously, nothing had been done to the house in years. Rory had lived in one room and even that was a wreck without a ceiling. The house was a dirty falling down mess. There was no central heating and it was freezing. It is really hard to imagine anybody living like that, but I loved him so it did not seem to matter. We used to sit and dream that one day when the music festival he organised became like Glastonbury we would live in luxury. He had bought me pate on toast to start with and sirloin steak for main course. We only ate the pate on toast and drank a lot of wine and then we made love...

Epilogue

My mental illness has spanned ten years now and every day I pray I am all right tomorrow. I have been misdiagnosed a lot of the time but I think eventually they have found a drug that suits my illness and I live with schizoid affective disorder and take Abilify. I now consider myself mentally ill and am very sorry for the pain I have inflicted upon my parents. As for my friends, they are a closed book, maybe one day they will find it in their hearts to forgive me for whatever I put them through. I do know I have a good family and with out them I do not know where I would be today. Above all I have learned it is to respect drugs and alcohol, or do not do them at all.

Who knows whether or not I would have been ill if I would never have touched them? My alcohol problem has also been resolved since meeting Rory I have given up alcohol and only have some on an occasion. I know I abused alcohol for a very long time and I am not proud of that. I lost everything to my mental illness, my life, my future and my friends and almost my family. I lost my status, self-respect and social standing. When I am ill, I lose my freedom, my driving licence, my responsibilities and my mind. If only I had taken my medication and faced up to my consequences, I would not have de-stabled so many people in ten years. I finished university and gained a 2;2 I'd hoped for a 2;1 but I wasn't lucky. I then took my UCPD 1 and 2 in screen writing at Teesside University too. I have not yet had any success with any of my plays but I live in hope. I enjoy writing so I keep on persevering and entering writing competitions.

From the moment my mother broke down at that meeting, I have solemnly taken my tablet daily and have never missed once. I am not affected by taking the tablet and I have been well for three years now without any interruption and I plan to stay that way, I have too much to lose if I get ill. I could not face six months in a mental institution, losing my son, losing my driving licence and so on, so if all I have to do is take the medicine then that is what I will do. I had a good CPN for two years who taught me a lot. She made me understand my warning signs and if I ever have any of them, I go straight for help. She also taught me about my chemical imbalance in my brain I produce too much dopamine and that is what makes me high. When it is explained scientifically, I do not think I sound like a loony, I just sound like someone who has something wrong with the functioning of his or her body.

I dated Rory for two years. I used to live at home during the week and then drive the long hour-long drive up to his remote farm in Wear dale every weekend. We have some great memories of our courtship and we also did up the house! For two years, I secretly took my tablet every night in the bathroom. Rory never suspected anything, in a way I deceived him for two years and when I told him I was mentally ill I broke down. I really had not wanted to tell him because I knew it would change his opinion of me forever. He was relaxed when I told him and we never really talk about it. I do not know whether it has changed us or not. We got married on St Patrick's Day 2006. Domini and I live in Wear dale now very happily. I am a full time mother and wife.

Rory has become an overnight success with his music festivals. I got myself a job too as the marketing and pr manager of the festival and I have been doing it for three years now. I work very hard and for once, I am good at what I do. It is nice to work for your husband.

Although I try not to think about my illness and the occult that surrounds it, I did lately find something very interesting on the Internet............ BLACK MAGIC, EVIL SPELLS, SUPERNATURAL INFLUENCES Black Magic, Evil Spells & Curses, Voodoo is the negative use of energies and powers by jealous and malicious beings of Kalyuga, whose main objective is to harm or deprive others of something, control their minds and influence them to do something specific or wrong/negative. It is the use of celestial powers for negative and evil purposes. Besides this, there are various other evil powers and negative energies like the Evil eye, Ghosts & Spirits, which are also very pro-active in Kalyuga. Evil eye is the sinister affect of a jealous mind with vicious intentions. Ghosts & Spirits are unsettled souls who have not reached their correct destination.

All the above Evil practices and Supernatural influences destroy the positive energies of the Cosmos, spread negativity, and give rise to depression, pessimism, evil thoughts, suicidal tendencies, mental diseases and imbalances on the one hand, and lack of peace, happiness and satisfaction on the other.

Black Magic can be used to harm or hurt a person by performing certain acts even at a far away place, and the effects can be experienced thousands of miles away. With the increase of jealousy, frustration, greed, selfishness, negativity and inability to tolerate other's happiness and growth, the use of Black Magic has become the most common way to take out one's vindictiveness and get sadistic satisfaction from the suffering and loss of others. This evil practice has increased a lot in the last few years, and many are suffering all over the world, very unaware of the attacks made by no other than their close friends, acquaintances and relatives. Many prosperous and happy families are ruined by Black magic.

Symptoms of Black Magic

Black Magic puts a block on a person's wisdom and intelligence, and all efforts to solve a problem go fruitless. One feels a mental block, gets negative thoughts and disturbed sleep with bad dreams. There is heaviness and weight on the heart, constriction in the chest, suffocation and stifling in the throat.

At times, there could suddenly be blue marks on thighs without getting hurt, faster heartbeat and erratic breathing without any physical exertion. There are quarrels in the family without any reason. One behaves in an abnormal and uncharacteristic manner. One has sudden fears and phobias, strange and weird experiences. One might feel the presence of somebody in the house, of being watched or followed.

One feels one is not getting one's due and can achieve much more. One is pessimistic and depressed, with lack of enthusiasm or desire to live and rise in life. One remains worried and tensed, never at peace, unable to relax, be happy, and lead a normal life.

Effects of Black Magic

Black Magic can play havoc with the life of the target person by destroying many aspects of his life, like sudden loss of wealth/prosperity, unexpected problems in business/profession, violent quarrels/fights in family, break-up of a relationship/marriage, prolonged illness, undiagnosed health troubles, destruction of mental peace & happiness, beauty & intelligence, mental unrest & inner turmoil, fears & phobias, uncharacteristic & abnormal behaviour. Black Magic can also result in repeated miscarriages, inability to enjoy sex or have children, without any deficiency, and unnatural deaths in the family in strange circumstances.

Black Magic can result in total destruction of the victim over a period of time. Black magic affects the circumstances and future prospects of a person, and destroys his Destiny, depriving him of what he was destined for. Even the best and most earnest of one's efforts result in failure, and one is unable to fulfil one's desires and get what one wants in life. Black Magic also affects the psyche of the victim in such a way that one looses the Will-power and mental energy to fight back or get out of the sinister situation one is in, and looses the desire to live or rise in life.

Black Magic becomes more chronic, dangerous and fatal with time, like a horrible disease that is left untreated. It spreads like a contagious disease, affecting the person's mind, brain, body, relationships, attitudes, work, money, marriage, career, and everything, which makes life worth living.

Curing Black Magic Spells

Putting a Black magic spell on someone is very easy for those knowing even a little bit about Spells and Tantrik art. However, to remove the Spell and eliminate its sinister effects needs lot of expertise', rigorous rituals and worship, years of knowledge, various 'Siddhis' & 'Sadhna'. Cure of Black magic and removal of Evil spells requires a high level of spiritual knowledge and psychic abilities as well as special Cosmic blessings of Deities & Nature.

Gurudev curses those doing Black Magic on innocent people and destroying their lives and happiness for years to come.

Black Magic

Gurudev's Talisman eradicates all ill effects of Black magic, Evil Spells, Curses, Ghosts & Spirits, and all such Supernatural influences and Sinister practices which are very active and common in Kalyuga, and which can ruin and destroy one's present and future life.

This Talisman not only removes all ill effects of past attacks, but also grants complete protection from any such future attacks. The wearer of this Talisman always remains immune from any Black magic attack or Evil spell.